IN A

QUIET GARDEN

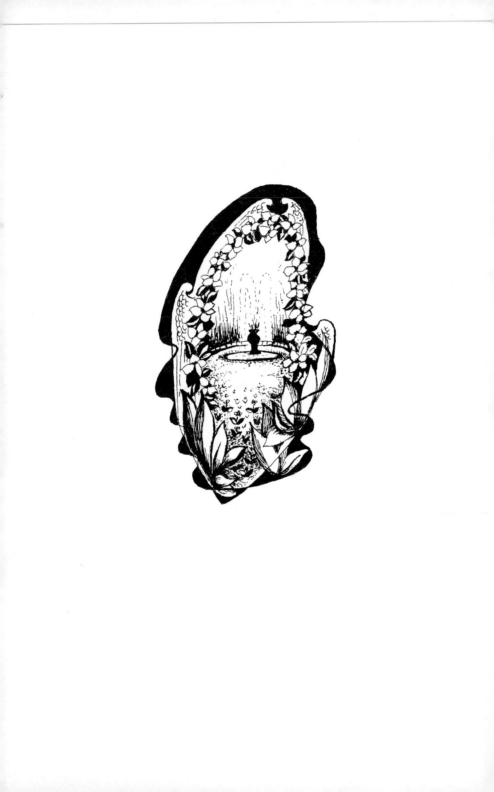

IN A QUIET

GARDEN

MEDITATIONS AND PRAYERFUL REFLECTIONS

by

Brigid Boardman and Philip Jebb

DOWNSIDE ABBEY

Downside Abbey Books
Stratton on the Fosse
Bath, England BA3 4RH
E-mail: books@downside.co.uk

© 2000:   Brigid Boardman
               Philip Jebb
               The Quiet Garden Trust

British Library Cataloguing in Publication Data:
A catalogue record of this book is available from
The British Library.

ISBN 1-898663-12-2

Typeset at Downside Abbey, Bath
Printed and Bound by Hobbs the Printers
Totton, Hampshire SO40 3WX

CONTENTS

Part III Additional Poems

PREFACE

by Esther de Waal

'Paradise' is the Greek word for a garden. And yet no sooner have our thoughts turned to the paradise of Eden than we of course discover that Paradise is not only a place of idyllic beauty and harmony but also one which holds dark and menacing forces, a place of sin and betrayal and suffering. It is therefore not so very surprising that since time immemorial gardens have given us images which present us with the whole universe in miniature, — and not least the universe which we ourselves carry within us. For gardens capture the imagination, and they have inspired poets, theologians, artists, and above all they have been a recurrent theme in the Bible and in the early Fathers. So we have an amazingly varied literary output which explores the riches which present themselves in a garden.

The Quiet Garden Movement has taken the fullness of the garden, both in its actual physical reality and in the images that it brings, and has made it the starting point for what has become a world-wide network. There are now gardens in many countries but all have this in common — they have become places in which to draw aside in order to encounter our own selves and encounter God in an oasis of calm, with space and time for silence, prayer and meditation. It began in 1992 with the intention of making gardens available as places of retreat, an idea so simple that one is tempted to say: why did this not happen before? The fact is that it *has* happened, and perhaps at a time when it was never more needed, for it is increasingly apparent that many people in today's world find themselves living with pressure and

1

anxiety and confusion. Some gardens are in places of incomparable loveliness, others are more modest, a small area staked out in the middle of urban development.

What then do they have in common? They ask us to take time, to slow down, to come with all our five senses alert and aware, and then in a state of mindfulness to be open to the vision of place, the visual rather than the verbal. But at the same time words can help, and should help. We turn to others, and we find ourselves stimulated by what they saw and what they felt. Sometimes this articulates what is already half-known or half-perceived; sometimes it is new and challenging, so that our own boundaries, our horizons are stretched and enriched. That is why this anthology is such a delight. It brings together a wide-ranging galaxy, some people whom we might expect to find here — for we immed-iately associate the name of Thomas Traherne with an almost intoxicated love of the natural world, and the name of Hildegard of Bingen with *veriditas*, greenness, but Rudyard Kipling and E. Nesbit and many others are unexpected companions. Each of us will pick our own treasures.

Time and again we are jolted into seeing anew, seeing afresh, seeing with wonder. 'One must look with the heart', says Antoine de Saint-Exupéry's *Little Prince*. We see with the totality of our whole selves, with the five senses. We recognise that we are surrounded by the Trinity of the three elements, earth, water, sun. Here is the interplay between the spiritual and the physical, God, nature, men and women enjoying that first harmony which there was at the start in the world which God created for humanity to live harmoniously with his creation. But that harmony asks of us our collaboration. Adam was sent out to till the ground, and that draws us

2

into a further development of the image of the garden: it means union between our work, the work of nature and God's work in guiding both. We are to share with God in the continuing, never-ending, unremitting work of collaboration: collaborating with the seasons, with the weather, the soil, the cycles of the moon. . . . But then, if I co-operate with the work and plan of God in the garden, so also I co-operate with his work and plan in my own life. The sense of inter-connectedness goes on growing the longer that I stay with these ideas. In the face of this mystery there is only one response and that is to move into the silence of meditation and prayer for, as the first of these meditations opens, 'prayer is the raising of the heart and mind to God, going out to God in love. . .'.

Having been associated with the Quiet Garden Movement I am so happy to have been asked to be associated with this book. It has given me pleasure, but more than that, it has helped me to see more clearly much that was half formed in my garden time. It is a book that I shall return to time and again, in gratitude; that I shall use when I am hard at work in my own garden, and I shall use when I stop and am at rest. It is then that I make the garden a place for silence and for meditation, for deepening my sense of the mystery of a God whose original act of creation of our humanity was set in a garden, and of whom the first question addressed to him as the Resurrected Son of God, the Redeemer of that same humanity, was 'Are you the gardener?'.

INTRODUCTION
by Brigid Boardman and Philip Jebb

The idea for our book came to each of us independently
— which was, we felt, a reason for regarding it as one
given to us for a purpose. Later this seemed to be con-
firmed by members of the Quiet Garden ministry who
had been wanting some such collection of meditations
appropriate for Quiet Garden Days.

We want the meditations to be as flexible as
possible in the way they are used. So the book is divided
into three parts. In the first, particular themes are
developed with the help of quotations from prose and
poetry, together with extracts from the Bible and the
Liturgy. In the second, the shorter reflective sentences
are likewise based on particular themes or ideas. Then in
the last part there are further quotations as suggestions
for additions or substitutions for the first.

Sometimes there are parallels between a theme in
each part, as, for example, in those based on the seasons.
Others remain distinct, those in the first part to be used
either by themselves for a shorter period or together with
one from the second for a longer one — when the two
themes may be related. It will be found that most of the
themes in each part harmonise together. Those from the
second are also more suited to a period of guided meditation.

Having described the contents of our book and
the way the meditations could be used, it is important to
add how they relate to the purpose of a Quiet Garden.
Such gardens vary widely in their outward characteristics
as to size, location and availability. But they all have
certain basic features in common. They offer spiritual
and physical renewal and refreshment in a safe envir-

onment and free from stress. But there is no hard-and-fast definition as to how these aims are achieved.

So at the start of a Quiet Garden Day it should be stressed that the meditations and their themes are offered as guides for those who find them helpful but with no obligation to follow them. We have found, however, that they fill a very positive role and can meet a real need for those whose lives are busy and stressful. They help to focus the mind and heart and so create that mood of receptive peace when prayer comes most readily. All prayer is the raising of the heart and mind to God, going out to God in love, acknowledging *his* love, *his* creative power, *his* holiness, his *JOY*. We can talk to God with ordinary words, our own or another's, but we can also just contem-plate God: look to him, receive from him. We can take to him our joys, works, sorrows and tempt-ations; sorrow for our failures, gratitude for his gifts, requests for the needs of ourselves and of the world.

One of the difficulties about praying can be the imagination, which may distract us with its activity. We do not pray with the imagination, but with our will and our understanding, but the imagination can 'get in the way', and lead us away from our prayer: if the image of someone who has hurt me comes into my consciousness and if I pay attention to this it can divert my will to anger and hatred of that person, and for as long as I continue in that state my prayer is lost.

For this reason many of the techniques of prayer are aimed at directing the imagination so that love and understanding, intention and attention, can remain centred on God. So the Rosary takes a 'picture' from the Gospels, e.g. the Angel Gabriel bringing the message to Mary, or the birth of Jesus in the stable at Bethlehem, and with the *help* of the imagination we are able to thank

God, worship God, get closer to the person of Jesus, get a better understanding of his message. If we come to realise that the imagination has wandered off to something else, we can gently bring it back to what we originally intended.

So in a garden it should not be difficult to direct our prayer through sights, sounds and scents to God's beautiful creation, to his love for all life, to his ordering of the universe, to his peace and joy.

We can recognise how the gardener co-operates with the work and plan of God and how we may do the same in our lives. Perhaps also think with sorrow of failures to co-operate or to respond to God's love and generosity. We can think of ugliness and the destruction of beauty outside the garden, which are powerful symbols of sin, and we then determine to work so that God's will be done on earth as it is in Heaven, our everlasting home.

And so we can come to true 'Contemplation', resting without words in God's beauty and peace.

Although this book is intended primarily for meditations in a Quiet Garden, it is hoped that others will find it helpful as well. There are those who cannot get to a Quiet Garden and there are many who do not have a garden of their own. But we all have another garden, a Garden of the Soul. From the earliest times, the soul has been likened to a garden and it is perhaps more valuable than ever today to 'cultivate' such an inner haven of peace. As we close this garden gate on our everyday cares we move along its paths reflecting on the themes and ideas presented here until we find the moment comes for silence and our encounter with the divine presence.

It is with this in mind that the book starts with the theme of 'The Garden of the Soul'.

PART I

by Brigid Boardman

— 1 —

THE GARDEN OF THE SOUL

Let us consider for a few minutes why the garden should have acquired this association as the *Garden of the Soul*.

The answer lies in the essential character of the actual garden as a place set apart and private. This is much more important than its appearance. A back-yard with some flower pots can serve as an image of the Garden of the Soul better than a great display of beauty.

This idea of privacy and enclosure forms the basis for the Soul as Garden. We 'retreat' within to a place we set apart where we can be quiet and attentive to the voice and presence of God.

This brings us to the second influence giving rise to the tradition: the Garden as Paradise. For in our Christian tradition, Paradise was the Garden of Eden, where God walked with us as our friend.

Although we lost that friendship, it has been restored through Christ. Our soul is therefore the place where we can encounter him, a 'Paradise within'.

There is, of course, a notable difference. Our *Garden of the Soul* is a flawed 'Paradise'. The serpent is never far from our Eden. But here the garden is again a perfect image. For the actual garden needs rain, frost, snow and all the ills of winter to create the spring and summer flowers and autumn fruit. So too when we are unable to feel anything but awareness of our weaknesses and sinfulness or of pain of any kind, the soul's Garden is still growing, gaining deeper roots in richer soil.

We do not need to think of the Garden of Eden as an actual place or the events there as historical. There is another kind of truth, expressed in myth and story, and in this sense the Genesis myth is as important for us now as it ever was.

There is a third aspect of the Garden we need to keep in mind. Unlike other places set apart, such as the country vale or woodland glade, or those scenes we associate with 'wilderness', the garden is the place where God, Man and Nature still enjoy a harmony we associate with the Garden of Eden as the way of life for which we were created. So in our Garden of the Soul we can be aware of our share in the divine life and at the same time and as part of it, in the life of the natural world. Today, more than ever, we need to recall this original harmony and reflect on it within ourselves.

Throughout the Old Testament the ideal way of life is described in terms of a city, a community, that would later evolve into the Church of the New Testament. But its attainment depends on the individual souls in their progress towards fulfilment; and here the descrip-tions are full of pastoral and garden imagery signifying the restoration of the original harmony between divine, natural and human life for which we were created:

> They shall come, shouting for joy
> on the mountain of Zion,
> Radiant for God's lavish gifts,
> for wheat, new wine and oil,
> the young sheep and cattle:
> They shall be like a watered garden,
> They will be sorrowful no more.[1]

Here is Isaiah's description of the good man who cares for his fellow-men:

> God will guide you always,
> will satisfy your needs in the desert;
> he will strengthen your bones
> and you will be like a watered garden,
> like an abundant spring
> whose waters will never fail.[2]

In the psalms there are many references to the souls of the just whose virtues bloom like plants in a garden but it is the Song of Songs which expresses this theme in the Old Testament most fully and beautifully. As a love poem it can be given different levels of meaning, but the underlying theme has been the accepted one for generations of mystics, for whom the Lover and the Bride are Christ and the Soul. We don't need to be mystics to respond to its language and the way it draws us into a union of divine, human and natural love that makes the garden imagery so essential to its theme.

Listen now to the Lover, Christ, as he addresses the Bride, the Soul:

> She is a garden enclosed,
> My sister, my bride:
> A garden enclosed,
> a fountain that is sealed.[3]

The Bride responds:

> Awake, north wind,
> and come, wind from the south!
> Breathe over my garden,
> to spread its sweet fragrance abroad.

Let my beloved come into his garden,
let him taste its choicest fruits.[4]

So the Lover accepts:

I come into my garden,
my sister, my bride.
I gather my myrrh and my spice,
I eat my honey from the comb,
I drink my wine and my milk.[5]

In the New Testament Jesus uses many images from growing things in his parables and sermons. He was of course familiar with the way these were used in the Hebrew Scriptures and I think these words of his which are no less familiar to us, take on a fresh beauty when we relate them to our theme:

Abide in me, as I in you.
As a branch cannot bear fruit by itself,
unless it remains with the vine,
neither can you unless you abide in me.
I am the vine,
you are the branches.
Whoever abides in me, and I in him,
He will bear fruit in plenty.[6]

The first Christians were already well aware of these associations in the teachings of Christ, which come together very early in the anonymous *Epistle to Diognetus* dating probably from the second century. According to this writer, each individual soul can become a Garden of Eden where the Trees of Life and of Knowledge no longer bring spiritual death but 'life-giving precepts of the truth'. And so:

They become a very paradise of delight, they make a
grove spring up and flourish within themselves, which
yields all manner of nourishment and adorns them
with fruit of every kind.[7]

Christ's resurrection in the garden has, from the earliest
times, given rise to the idea of Christ as a Gardener of the
soul. The fourth-century saint, Paulinus of Nola, made
a garden where he could retire and meditate. He wrote
on this theme to a friend:

So ensure by your prayers that the highest Father of
the household and the heavenly Husbandman and the
careful Gardener attend, haunt, and mark out the
garden of my soul like the one in which He taught,
prayed and rose again.[8]

I particularly like this idea of the unkempt Garden of the
Soul, much in need of the attention of the 'careful
Gardener'.

Saint Teresa of Avila devoted a large part of her
autobiography to describing the soul's progress in terms
of the planting and care of a garden where Christ is the
Gardener:

The beginner must think of himself as of one setting
out to make a garden in which the Lord is to take his
delight, yet in soil most unfruitful and full of weeds.
His Majesty uproots the weeds and will set good
plants in their stead . . . It used to give me great
delight to think of my soul as a garden and of the Lord
as walking in it. I would beg him to increase the
fragrance of the little buds of virtue which seemed to
be beginning to appear and to keep them alive so that
they might bloom to his glory . . . And I would ask
him to prune away any of them he wished to, for I
knew that the plants would be all the better if he did.[9]

To conclude these reflections and lead on to our time for meditation here are some extracts from a sequence of meditations on *The School of the Heart* by the seventeenth-century poet Francis Quarles:

> See how this dry and thirsty land,
> Mine heart, doth gaping, gasping stand,
> And, close below, opens towards Heav'n and thee;
> Thou Fountain of felicity,
> Great Lord of living waters, water me:
> Let not my breath, that pants with pain,
> Waste and consume itself in vain.

> Thou boundless Ocean of grace,
> Let thy free Spirit have a place
> Within my heart: full rivers then, I know,
> Of living waters, forth will flow;
> And all thy plants, thy fruits, thy flow'rs will grow.
> Whilst thy springs their roots do nourish
> They must needs be fair, and flourish.

The Heart — or Soul — has first been tilled and then planted by God. At last the flowers appear:

> Faith is a fruitful grace;
> Well planted, stores the place,
> Fills all the borders, beds, and bow'rs,
> With wholesome herbs and pleasant flow'rs:
> Great Gardener, thou say'st it, and I believe,
> What thou dost mean to gather, thou wilt give.
> Take then mine heart in hand, to fill't,
> And it shall yield thee what thou wilt.
> Yea thou, by gath'ring more,
> Shall still increase my store.[10]

— 2 —

THE HARMONY OF THE GARDEN

What do we mean by 'harmony'? *The Oxford Dictionary* defines it as 'forming a consistent or agreeable whole' — so when we apply it to our gardens we find it describes well the union between our work, the work of nature and God's work guiding both. Divine, human and natural life come together in the garden in a way that is not quite the same anywhere else.

It is no wonder, then, that according to the Biblical story the history of the human race originated in a garden setting:

> And the Lord God planted a garden in Eden, in the east; and there he put the man he had fashioned. Out of the soil God made to grow every tree that is pleasant to the sight and good to eat. . . . And God took the man and put him in the garden of Eden to till it and care for it.[11]

We do not have to believe in the historical validity of the Genesis story since it has the validity of myth, communicating truths which elude our rational understanding. Down the ages the story has evoked responses from all aspects of human thought and art. But what we need to remember here is surprisingly simple although too often overlooked. The Hebrew word translated as 'till' or 'work' also has the implication 'to serve' while 'keep' is more accurately translated as 'caring' or 'preserving'.[12]

The command given to Adam is the command to Everyman: to offer service to the land, to care for and preserve it and then to reap its fruits and enjoy its blessings. It is a two-way process, the true meaning of the 'dominion' of humanity over the rest of creation. We have a special role as created in God's image but just because of this image we must emulate the care and love of him whose image we bear.

This, then, is the fuller meaning of the harmony of the garden. Here we do indeed serve and care for our patch of soil and the plants we grow and watch over, carrying out the first injunction given to the human race to work in harmony with nature and in compliance with the divine ordering of both human and natural life..

As gardeners we come closest to the caring and preserving presence of God in his creation. If we are not actual gardeners but respond to the message of the garden, then we are no less close to the same presence.

In the Bible, the role of gardener is often synonymous with that of the farmer, before agriculture lost its simple adherence to the basic principles that still direct our gardening activities. Again and again in the Old Testament God's loving care for his people is described in terms of caring and preserving the land:

> You care for the earth and water it,
> you greatly enrich it;
> the river of God overflows,
> to provide your people with grain:
> for thus you have prepared it.
> You water its furrows abundantly,
> levelling its ridges,
> softening it with showers,
> and blessing its growth.[13]

As constantly the same care extends throughout the created world:

You make the grass grow for the cattle,
and plants for all our needs,
to bring forth food from the earth,
and wine to gladden our hearts,
oil to make the face shine,
and bread to strengthen the heart.
The trees of the Lord are well watered,
the cedars of Lebanon he planted,
in them the birds build their nests;
in the fir tree the stork makes its home.[14]

The dependence of the people on God's preservation of the land is even described in terms of the original garden. 'Eden' means 'delight' and the prophets took the name to represent the fulfilment of the promise of salvation:

The Lord will bring comfort to Zion;
He will comfort her even in the desert,
make her wilderness ordered like Eden,
her wastes like the Lord's own garden;
Joy and gladness will be found in her,
thanksgiving and the sound of song.[15]

So too, there is the constant reminder of God's purpose, his guiding 'word' as the seed in the hand of the sower:

For as the rain and the snow come down from the heavens and do not return without watering the earth, — making it yield and sprout, giving seed to the sower and bread for those who would eat — so shall my word be that goes forth from my mouth. It shall not return to me empty, but shall accomplish all that I purpose.[16]

In the New Testament Christ carries on this traditional view of God's presence in our lives and the life of the world about us. We are familiar with the images in the parable of the sower, the mustard seed that becomes a great tree, the tares that must grow with the wheat until the harvest, the secret growth of the seed likened to the working of grace in the soul and in the Church. God as the gardener-farmer is especially clear in Christ's word to the pharisees: 'Any plant which my father in heaven has not planted will be rooted up'.[17]

Down the centuries the garden has continued to represent an original harmony between God, man and nature which was increasingly hard to recover in any other environment. I believe this is the real reason for the present appeal of all aspects of gardens and gardening today, spanning classes and cultures. We sense that here we are in touch with a meaning in life which is threatened as never before. We feel helpless at the onset of effects of our civilization which look set to destroy not only that civilization but the life-forces on which we depend for the necessities of our existence. It is a disruption between divine, human and natural life that we fear, whatever the terminology used to describe our present threatened environment.

We tend to regard our fears as having developed as the result of our recent abuse of the natural world and its resources. So it is quite a surprise to find such fears expressed as early as the twelfth century. Hildegard of Bingen was a Benedictine Abbess whose understanding of the relationship between science and nature was well ahead of her time and only now beginning to be recognised. Her profound awareness of the harmony of creation also found expression in songs and poems — but it could lead her to a terrible awareness of what could happen when that harmony is violated:

Now in the people
that were meant to be green,
there is no more life of any kind.
There is only shrivelled barrenness.

The winds are burdened
by the utterly awful stink of evil,
selfish goings-on.

Thunderstorms menace.

The air belches out
the filthy uncleanliness of the peoples.

There pours forth
a loathsome darkness,
that withers the green,
and wizens the fruit
that was to serve as food for the people.

Sometimes this layer of air
is full,
full of a fog that is the source
of many destructive and barren creatures,
that destroy and damage the earth,
rendering it incapable
of sustaining humanity.
. . .
The high,
the low,
all of creation,
God gives to humankind to use.

If this privilege is misused,
God's justice permits creation to
punish humanity.

Yet for Hildegard, despite her fearfully prophetic vision, this is not the end. It is we who bring the punishment on ourselves but God has the ultimate authority to transform the resulting suffering. Her lines here cannot be bettered as the way into our meditation on the true message of the harmony of the garden as we have listened to it so far:

God desires
that all the world
be pure in his sight.

The earth should not be injured.
The earth should not be destroyed.

As often as the elements,
the elements of the world,
are violated
by ill-treatment,
so God will cleanse them.

God will cleanse them
thru the sufferings,
thru the hardships
of humankind.[18]

THE GARDEN IN MAY: THE MONTH OF MARY

May is the month of spring's fullest expression of birth and new life. So it is not surprising that from the early years of the Church it has been the month dedicated to Mary. Following on from this, it is also most appropriate that at this time we think of her especially in her role of Mother.

We love and honour her as Mother of Christ and so too as our Mother, Mother of the human race. But today I want to reflect on her role as Mother of the Created World. This is not one we hear nearly so much about but I am very sure that this will be changing as we become more aware of the way human and natural life depend on one another and both on a life that exists beyond either. As Mother of Christ and Mother of the human race she unites divine and human life. It must surely follow that she likewise embraces the life of the rest of the natural world as no less God's creation. There is perhaps a tendency to avoid this aspect of her Motherhood as in some way linked to New Age ideas about earth goddesses and similar seeming aberrations of the Christian tradition. Whereas I believe we need to regard such ideas as signs of a search for the truths which earlier beliefs were foreshadowing.

Although it is an aspect of Mary's role that we need today in a special way, we are reviving an ancient tradition which we can hear already clearly expressed as early as the eleventh century in a sermon by Saint Anselm:

Blessed Lady, sky and stars, earth and rivers, day and night — everything that is subject to the power or use of man — rejoice that through you they are in some sense restored to their lost beauty and are endowed with inexpressible new grace . . . The universe rejoices with new and indefinable loveliness. Not only does it feel the unseen presence of God himself, its Creator, it sees him openly, working and making it holy. These great blessings spring from the blessed fruit of Mary's womb . . .

Lady, full and overflowing with grace, all creation receives new life from your abundance. Virgin blessed above all creatures, through your blessing all creation is blessed . . . God created all things, and Mary gave birth to God. The God who made all things gave himself form through Mary, and thus he made his own creation. He who could create all things from nothing would not remake his own creation without Mary.

God, then, is the Father of the created world and Mary the Mother of the re-created world. God is the Father by whom all things were given life, and Mary the mother through whom all things were given new life . . .

Truly the Lord is with you, to whom the Lord granted that all creatures should owe as much to you as to himself.[19]

By the twelfth century Mary's role as Mother is more clearly identified with spring-time fertility, given outward expression in the beauties of the natural world. Hildegard of Bingen whose ideas we have already noted (see p.16) was also an artist, but above all it is her poetry that celebrates her delight in God's creation and his presence within it. So in one of her Songs, 'De Sancta Maria', she rejoices in the Motherhood of Mary as inseparable from the renewal of springtime life:

Hail to you, O greenest, most fertile branch!
You budded forth amidst breezes and winds
in search of the knowledge of all that is holy.
When the time was ripe
your own branch brought forth blossoms.
Hail, greetings to you!
The heat of the sun exudes sweat from you
like the balsam's perfume.
In you, the most stunning flower has blossomed
and gives off its sweet odour
to all the herbs and roots,
which were dry and thirsting before your arrival.
Now they spring forth in fullest green!
Because of you, the heavens give dew to the grass,
the whole Earth rejoices;
Abundance of grain comes from Earth's womb
and on its stalks and branches the birds nest.
And because of you, nourishment is given
to the human family
and great rejoicing to those gathered round the table.
And so in you, O gentle Virgin,
is every fullness of joy, everything that Eve rejected.
Now let endless praise resound to the Most High![20]

'Because of you . . . the whole Earth rejoices'. What a
perfect way to describe May as Mary's month. But there
are others as perfect though different, reaching down to
our own day. To lead into our meditation time I have
chosen the 'May Magnificat' by Gerard Manley Hopkins,
one of the few poets who have celebrated the Incarnation
in terms of the bond between human life and that of the
natural world. For him, Mary is the great exemplar of
this bond and his poem is especially right for a May
Quiet Garden Day:

May is Mary's month, and I
Muse at that and wonder why:
     Her feasts follow reason,
     Dated due to season —

Candlemas, Lady Day;
But the Lady Month, May,
     Why fasten that upon her,
     With a feasting in her honour?

Is it only its being brighter
Than the most are must delight her?
     Is it opportunist
     And flowers findest soonest?

Ask of her, the mighty mother:
Her reply puts this other
     Question: What is Spring? —
     Growth in everything —

Flesh and fleece, fur and feather,
Grass and greenworld all together;
     Star-eyed strawberry-breasted
     Throstle above her nested

Cluster of busie blue eggs thin
Forms and warms the life within;
     And bird and blossom swell
     In sod or sheath or shell.

All things rising, all things sizing
Mary sees, sympathising,
     With that world of good,
     Nature's motherhood.
Their magnifying of each its kind
With delight calls to mind
     How she did in her stored
     Magnify the Lord.

Well but there was more than this:
Spring's universal bliss
    Much, had much to say
    To offering Mary May.

When drop-of-blood-and-foam-of-dapple
Bloom lights the orchard apple
    And thicket and thorp are merry
    With silver-surfèd cherry

And azuring-over greybell makes
Wood banks and brakes wash wet like lakes
    And magic cuckoocall
    Caps, clears, and clinches all —

This ecstasy all through mothering earth
Tells Mary her mirth till Christ's birth
    To remember and exultation
    In God who was her salvation.[21]

SPRING IN THE GARDEN

Spring is the season that arouses our emotions more than any other. We feel the sap rise in our bodies as we know it is rising in the world about us. In the garden the waking to new life is even more poignant because so much more a part of our everyday experience. As we witness it in the first green spikes and the first tiny sign of the snowdrop there come moments when our everyday life and experience are transformed by a sense of wonder which at other times and seasons we too often neglect and miss.

Many poets have attempted to capture this compelling of the spirit to become aware of the wonder of renewed life. We cannot do better at the start of our spring meditation than listen to the voices of two very different poets in their response to the springtime of life. The first is by Eleanor Farjeon and may be known to you as a hymn rather than a poem:

> Morning has broken!
> like the first morning,
> blackbird has spoken
> like the first bird.
> Praise for the singing!
> Praise for the morning!
> Praise for them, springing
> fresh from the Word!
>
> Sweet the rain's new fall
> sunlit from heaven,
> like the first dew fall
> on the first grass.

Praise for the sweetness
of the wet garden,
sprung in completeness
where his feet pass.

Mine is the sunlight!
Mine is the morning
born of the one light
Eden saw play!
Praise with elation,
praise ev'ry morning,
God's re-creation
of the new day![22]

The second poem is from 'The Heart's Journey' by
Siegfried Sassoon:

As I was walking in the gardens where
Spring touched the brooms with green, stole over me
A sense of wakening leaves that filled the air
With boding of Elysian days to be.

Cold was the music of the birds; and cold
The sunlight, shadowless with misty gold:
It seemed I stood with Youth on the calm verge
Of some annunciation that should bring
With flocks of silver angels, ultimate Spring
Whence all that life had longed for might emerge.[23]

The first poem evokes the morning freshness of a spring
garden with that sudden sense of springtime joy such as
we may experience only rarely but it can be at any time
in our lives. It passes all too quickly, leaving a memory of
sweetness tinged with that sadness which is the essence
of the second poem.

As soon as we are of an age to respond to the
message of spring in its freshness and beauty we are also

of an age to be aware of that sadness, a kind of poignancy which I doubt if any art has been able fully to express. It is, in essence, the longing of the human spirit for that perfection of life which we know we can never attain and yet for which we have a deep largely unconscious conviction we were created to enjoy. That is why springtime is so closely linked with the Eden myth with all its rich store of the truth contained in myth. And our actual gardens share in that truth: their snowdrops and crocuses and daffodils arouse memories of innocence and freshness we associate with the first Garden, with a perfection of which we are only aware as a loss.

For there has to be an accompanying sense of pain that spring is only a brief prelude to the continuing process of life and death. We cannot hold it back or make it our own — any more than we can hold back the course of our life's span.

We will only make it our own when we have passed beyond the cycle of human and natural life. In our meditation we can allow this further truth to take over from those other responses to spring. Then gradually the combined joy and pain evoked by our springtime garden can lead into a single prayer: that together they will lead us to retain within the Garden of our Soul the promise of 'ultimate joy'.

We have associated both the joy and the pain with the fresh beauty of the spring garden. But we miss a vital element in the season of new life if we only think of it in such a context. The sap rises everywhere, in the city back yard and the hospital ward no less than in the scenes evoked by our two poems. So here to end and to lead on to our meditation is another evocation of spring as we share in the response of the office workers to Caryll Houselander's 'Tree in the City':

At last on the little black tree
in the city square,
There is a green leaf.

Hesitating,
a ray of the sun comes down.
It is a white finger of light,
Pointing to life.

In the offices,
The row of pale faces are lifted,
They are turned to the green spark,
Unlit candles, wistful for flame.

They are not dreaming,
merely of the distant countryside,
Of passing loveliness.
They know, that loveliness
Runs out, even through privileged hearts,
Like sand through an hour glass.
They want to begin to live,
And to live for ever.

The spark of life
In each of their souls
Is a gem in a locked casket.
It suddenly burns more brightly,
Waxes and wanes
Like a breathing ember.

Now it could be fanned into a great flame, by
a mere breath.
Will no one come,
Into the city of London,
With the gift of his breath,
To answer
The people's wordless supplication
For Life?[24]

The question need not diminish our own springtime mood but it can direct the sadness we have found accompanying the sweetness. It is too easy to think only of how both affect ourselves, evoking memories, perhaps, of childhood days when it seemed there was no cloud to shadow our blue skies. Or memories of later days when clouds obscured the light and spring had little meaning for us. This poem turns us away from our own joy or sorrow to recall the much wider seasonal rebirth we share with those for whom it is only manifested in the tree outside the office window. Let us move into our meditation with thanksgiving for our garden setting and a prayer for those who cannot share it with us.

— 5 —

SUMMER IN THE GARDEN

To set the scene for our summer meditation, here are
some verses on the theme of sunshine and shadow:

> How beautiful the shadows all about me,
> That lie so softly on my garden lawn,
> And mingle with the golden gleams of sunlight,
> This palpitating, perfect summer morn.
>
> How beautiful to dream, all toil forgetting,
> For this brief hour to dream in restful ease,
> To feel the creeping sun and shade about me,
> And listen to the happy noise of bees!
>
> Just there beneath the great dark cedar branches,
> The richest, deepest shadow of them all!
> But even gayest roses have their shadow;
> Even the baby bird upon the wall.
>
> Come silent shadows, wrap your strength about me,
> If I, by chance, should find the sunny way,
> My garden plot were not so dear without thee,
> This satisfying, perfect summer day.[25]

This description of a summer morning in the garden
depends on the contrast between the shimmering heat
and the deep shade. Shadow is so often linked in our
minds with gloom and fear and even death: yet anyone
who has experienced the unrelenting heat of the summer
sun knows the relief shade brings, with the sense of
returning life to exhausted limbs. Sunshine and shadow
are equally essential to the life of the natural world and
especially in the hot summer months. Sunshine ripens

and matures but requires the slowing-down process of shade, without which our plants could dry up and burn away. Furthermore, we water them when they are in the shade which provides the right response from soil and roots.

Their counterparts are equally essential to the life of the human spirit, so closely are we interleaved, as it were, with the rest of creation. And when we have reached the summer season of life we are better able to recognise this truth about the place of sunshine and shade in human experience. We no longer expect and demand that life treats us as we expect and intend. We have learned that the light and dark in our lives can no more be controlled than the sunshine and shadow in our gardens. It is when we reach this summer season in life that we respond to the lesson in one of two ways. We can reject and resist or we can accept and affirm it. That is why the long summer days in our life are so important and take up so many of the years of our life-span. The lesson takes a long time and many efforts of acceptance before we can absorb it and fully comprehend it.

The sunshine days of achievement and satisfaction must be accompanied by the shadow days of frustration and monotony. It is only when both are accepted as equally part of our maturing lives that we can relax and enjoy a peace that we then share with the fruitful peace of the summer garden.

There is a poem by the seventeenth-century poet George Herbert which seems to me to express this need for acceptance of both sunshine and shadow in our lives. In the poem he is weighed down by the sense of his past sins and shortcomings, to which he feels sure he will return. Then he experiences relief and joy as he becomes aware of God's love and unfailing forgiveness. These alternating spiritual periods of sunshine and shadow are probably known to most of us. Accepting both as equally part of our drawing closer to God is the chief lesson we can learn from the garden scene with which we set out. As in George Herbert's poem, we may not now enjoy the years of springtime flowers and greenness. But we are filled with gratitude that even so, after the tempests in life comes renewal and we 'bud again'. It is a constantly recurring process of darkness and light, tempest and calm, until at last we are within sight of the garden where the tempest cannot reach and the flowers will never fade. Here, then is 'The Flower' by George Herbert:

How fresh, O Lord, how sweet and clean
Are thy returns! E'en as the flowers in Spring;
To which, besides their own demesne,
The late-past frosts tribute of pleasure bring.
Grief melts away
Like snow in May,
As if there were no such cold thing.

Who would have thought my shrivelled heart
Could have recovered greenness? It was gone
Quite under ground; as flowers depart
To see their mother-root, when they have blown,
Where they together
All the hard weather,
Dead to the world, keep house unknown.

These are thy wonders, Lord of power,
Killing and quick'ning, bringing down to Hell
And up to heaven in an hour;
Making a chiming of a passing-bell.
We say amiss,
This or that is:
Thy word is all, if we could spell.

O that I once past changing were,
Fast in thy Paradise, where no flower can wither.
Many a spring I shoot up fair,
Offering at Heaven. Growing and groaning thither;
Nor doth my flower
Want a spring-shower,
My sins and I joining together.

But while I grow in a straight line,
Still upwards bent, as if Heaven were mine own,
Thy anger comes, and I decline:
What frost to that? what pole is not the zone,
Where all things burn,
When thou dost turn,
And the least frown of thine is shown?

And now in age I bud again,
After so many deaths I live and write;
I once more smell the dew and rain,
And relish versing: O my only Light
It cannot be
That I am he
On whom thy tempests fell all night.

These are thy wonders, Lord of love,
To make us see we are but flowers that glide;
Which when we once can find and prove,
Thou hast a garden for us, where to bide;
Who would be more,
Swelling through store,
Forfeit their Paradise by their pride.[26]

6

AUTUMN IN THE GARDEN

There are many ways to reflect on this season of thanksgiving and fulfilment which, though distinct, are closely related.

We can think of it as a time of fulfilment in harvest and in thanksgiving, reminding us of our dependence on God's providence in his creation.

Such fulfilment leads on to the folding-down process of the weeks of later autumn, reaching out towards the calm of a day's end — or the end of a life.

The fulfilment is not an end in itself. It contains within it the seed of springtime life. The folding down, the falling leaves, is a folding over of the life of the seed in the earth. It is the protection of new life to grow in the earth as the human seed is protected to grow in the dark safety of the womb.

With these ideas in mind and to settle our thoughts into an autumn mood of gratitude and fulfilment, I have chosen a poem by Edward Hayes. He links the season with fulfilment as associated with retirement from work and with gratitude as expressed in contentment. In this way he brings the season into our own human experience of life in our autumn years:

O sacred season of Autumn, be my teacher,
     for I wish to learn the virtue of contentment.
As I gaze upon your full-coloured beauty,
     I sense all about you
     an at-homeness with your amber riches.

You are the season of retirement,
     of full barns and harvested fields.
The cycle of growth has ceased,
     and the busy work of giving life
     is now completed.
I sense in you no regrets:
     you've lived a full life.

I live in a society that is ever-restless,
     always eager for more mountains to climb,
     seeking happiness through more and more
     possessions.
As a child of my culture
     I am seldom truly at peace with what I have.
Teach me to take stock of what I have given and
                         received;
     may I know that it's enough,
     that my striving can cease
     in the abundance of God's grace.
May I know the contentment
     that allows the totality of my energies
     to come to full flower.
May I know that like you I am rich beyond measure.

As you, O Autumn, take pleasure in your great beauty,
     let me also take delight
     in the abundance of the simple things in life
     which are the true source of joy.
With the golden glow of peaceful contentment
     may I truly appreciate this autumn day. [27]

The poem is a prayer to be made aware of our blessings, whether of the autumn season or the autumn in our lives. Thanksgiving is an underlying theme for autumn as the time we associate with the harvest thanksgiving festivals. If we are in America there is the Thanksgiving feast itself — which among the early settlers arose from giving thanks for the blessings of their new land and in many ways was based on the harvest festivals they had left behind.

There is, of course, the reverse side as there always has to be in our fallen world. God working through his creation provides amply for the whole human race. It is we who through our selfishness and greed have upset the natural balance. Our responsibilities towards the peoples who suffer in consequence should be more present to us at this season of gratitude for the natural riches we enjoy.

Such reminders can lead us on to be more aware of our common humanity and our common dependence on the life of the natural world. And coming from the world-wide scene to our own garden scene we can feel it more poignantly. The flowers and fruits we sowed and watched grow to fulfilment must now fade and fall. We cannot avoid the similar process in our own experience of life; but autumn brings us a promise beyond the falling leaves and the diminishments of age. The promise of renewal, whether of the seasons or the spirit, is always with us and never more than at this time. It lies at the heart of all our thanksgivings for present blessings and leads us on through the enfolding months of darkness to come.

This sharing of the autumns in our lives with the life of the natural world is beautifully expressed in the following lines by Hildegard of Bingen, the twelfth-century Benedictine Abbess whom we have already met in Chapters 2 and 3. It is her poems on the human spirit and our sharing in the life of the natural world which lead on to meditative prayer:

> When in the fullness of its time
> this creation wilts,
> its vigour returns to its own source.
>
> This is the underlying natural law.
> When the elements of the world fulfil
> their function,
> they come to ripeness
> and their fruit is gathered back to God.
>
> Now these things
> are in reference to the soul's life:
> spiritual vitality is alive in the soul
> in the same way as the marrow of the
> hips in the flesh.
>
> Out of the soul in good standing,
> the vigour of the virtues flows out
> as do the elements of creation,
> it flows back in the same capacity
> in attentive prayer.[28]

7

WINTER IN THE GARDEN

Let us start our reflections on winter with lines that set a scene with which we are all too familiar, the scene where winter brings in death. My scene metaphor is intentional because the lines are Shakespeare's:

> That time of year thou mayst in me behold
> When yellow leaves, or none, or few, do hang
> Upon those boughs which shake against the cold,
> Bare ruined choirs where late the sweet birds sang.
> In me thou seest the twilight of such day
> As after sunset fadeth in the west,
> which by and by black night doth take away,
> death's second self, that seals up all the rest.
> In me thou seest the glowing of such fire
> That on the ashes of his youth doth lie,
> As the deathbed whereon it must expire,
> Consumed with that which it was nourished by.
> This thou perceiv'st, which makes thy
>   love more strong,
>   To love that well which thou must leave
>   ere long.[29]

As so often, Shakespeare here captures a universal human mood. We fear old age and we fear death and both are inseparable from our responses to the winter season. Cold, darkness, barrenness . . . and it is still the season when, despite our modern medicine, death comes more readily than at any other.

Yet from centuries before Christ, the midwinter solstice had become the Feast of Light. The turning-point of the natural year, binding earth with the movement of the heavens, became also a turning-point for the human spirit — so closely are our lives, at all levels, interwoven with the web of creation.

Christmas has baptised the ancient rites of the midwinter feast but the associations remain. Candles and stars are the great symbols of light to which we all respond, whatever our religious background or lack of it.

Light in darkness, life in death. This is the message of winter, for the natural world and for ourselves. And it is also the paradox at the heart of our Christian belief, linking the new-born Christ-Child with the crucified and risen Christ in ways that defy our rational minds to explain and leave us open only to the mystery of the seed that appears from the earth to become the mighty tree. So also we have that other great winter symbol of the Christmas Tree with the lights that again recall the Christmas message.

Until we can enter into this paradox and make it our own it remains no more than a 'truism' or perhaps a useful appendage for a Christmas sermon. To help us here we will listen to the direction suggested by the great French scientist and mystic Pierre Teilhard de Chardin when he writes of what he calls our 'diminishments'. They are the seemingly negative and destructive happenings in our lives that reach a climax as we approach death:

> It is easy enough to understand that God can be grasped in and through every life. But can God also be found in and through every death? This is what perplexes us deeply. And yet this is what we must learn to acknowledge as a matter of settled habit and practice . . . Unless we are prepared to forfeit commerce with God in one of the most widespread and at the same time most profoundly passive and

receptive experiences of human life.

. . . We must overcome death by finding God in it. And by the same token, we shall find the divine established in our innermost hearts, in the last stronghold which might have seemed able to escape His reach.[30]

In the context of these words it is clear that we are asked to enter the experience of death as we find it in the diminishments of our everyday lives with their outer and inner trials and troubles. We cannot anticipate our actual death, either its circumstances or its timing. But by habitually recognising and accepting our human limitations, our failures and frustrations, we are open to finding God within them. Accordingly, the habit becomes, largely unconsciously, our preparation for the final acceptance whenever and however it comes.

Here, then, we find the winter message bringing us the greatest promise of all which is also the Christian promise. By accepting the diminishments of the dying year, the dark furrow, we become aware of the soil as preparing for the seeds of renewal — not only in the natural cycle of death and life but in our own supernatural cycle where death leads on to another no less real dimension of life.

In our gardens, winter is teaching us how nature accepts the cold and darkness as the essential preparation for spring. So now I want to conclude these reflections by drawing them together in a way which needs some explanation. I have chosen passages from that childhood's classic 'The Secret Garden'. The appeal of the story is so widespread and spans the century's generations because it touches chords within our memories that go deeper than childhood recollections.

Behind the story itself is the life in death message of the winter season that is central to the theme and its outcome.

A lonely child, withdrawn into herself through lack of love, discovers the Secret Garden on a winter afternoon that is as cold as her own feeling for life has become. As she enters the Garden and gradually discovers the life hidden beneath the seeming deadness of the rose branches, the transformation begins that will bring spring for herself and those she will draw likewise into the Garden — no longer a hidden Secret Garden but still embracing the essential secret of returning life which we can find in all our gardens.

Here, then is Mary as she first discovers 'the sweetest, most mysterious-looking place anyone could imagine' with its tangle of bare branches and desolate rose bushes:

> Everything was strange and silent and she seemed to be hundreds of miles away from anyone, but somehow she did not feel lonely at all. All that troubled her was her wish that she knew whether all the roses were dead. . . She did not want it to be a quite dead garden. If it were a quite alive garden, how wonderful it would be, and what thousands of roses would grow on every side. . .
>
> There seemed to have been grass paths here and there, and in one or two corners there were alcoves of evergreen with stone seats or tall moss-covered flower urns in them. As she came near the second of these alcoves she stopped skipping. There had once been a flower bed in it, and she thought she saw something sticking out of the black earth — some sharp little pale green points . . . 'Yes, they are tiny growing things and they might be crocuses or snowdrops or daffodils', she whispered. She bent very close to them and sniffed

the fresh scent of the damp earth . . .

'It isn't quite a dead garden', she cried out softly to herself. 'Even if the roses are dead, there are other things alive'.[31]

As we learn later, the roses are very much alive. The garden mirrors Mary's own inner life in its winter cold and seeming deadness to feeling. But there are the secret signs of spring as there are in Mary's own heart as she responds to them. The story unfolds towards the spring that spreads from the garden to herself and to those who through her are touched by the same message.

From here it is only a short step to our meditation on the message of our winter garden. It will draw us on towards spring but now with the acceptance of the present scene that represents those diminishments we have also to accept in life. Then we, too, may find our garden scene has become our own Secret Garden.

— 8 —

AT WORK IN THE GARDEN

To start our reflections on gardening as a subject for meditation I have chosen the charming and light-hearted instructions left us by Thomas Tusser from the sixteenth century. His rather doggerel-like verses do not seem quite appropriate — until we select some features that may not be apparent at the first reading.

In March and in April, from morning to night,
    in sowing and setting, good huswives delight:
To have in a garden, or other like plot,
    to turn up their house, and to furnish their pot.

The nature of flowers dame Physick doth shew,
    she teacheth them all to be knowne to a few.
To set or to sowe, or else sowne to remove,
    how that should be practised, learne if ye love.
. . .
At spring (for the summer) sowe garden ye shall,
    at harvest (for winter) or sowe not at all.
Oft digging, removing, and weeding (ye see),
    makes herbes the more holesome and greater to bee.

Time faire, to sowe or to gather be bold,
    but set or remove when the weather be cold.
Cut all thing or gather, the Moone in the wane,
    but sowe in encreasing, or give it his bane.

Now set doo aske watering with pot or with dish,
    new sowne doo not so, if ye doo as I wish.
Through cunning with dible, rake, mattock, and spade,
    by line and by leaven, trim garden is made.

Who soweth too lateward, hath seldome good seed,
 who soweth too soone, little better shall speed.
Apt time and the season so divers to hit,
 let aier and laier helpe practise and wit.[32]

(For 'aier' we read weather and for 'laier', the soil.) On reflection, the first aspect of Tusser's verses that comes to mind is the fact that his instructions could have been written today. There is a timelessness about gardening that sets it apart from agricultural work and even from commercial market gardening — where new inventions and treatments are constantly challenging older methods. But Tusser's 'dible, rake, mattock, and spade' are as essential tools for us as they were for him. Similarly, his more general directions are equally valid as the time to sow and to prune, to dig and to weed.

  Secondly, at the outset he regards the adornment of the home, 'to turn up the house' as hardly less important than 'to furnish the pot'. Beauty and utility: both are essential to the uses of the garden.

  Over and above these considerations, there is the underlying sense that the housewife-gardener is working in constant collaboration with the natural world — with the seasons, the cycles of the moon, the weather and the type of soil in her garden. She must direct her efforts in accordance with their dictates or her efforts will be of no lasting value.

  It is a short step from here to reflecting on how gardening has from the first been identified as the occupation that can draw us closest to God's presence at work in the world. When Adam was ordered to 'till and to keep' the first garden, his tasks were not far removed from our gardening today. And according to the biblical narrative, the Garden of Eden was a place of beauty as well as utility — representing with the truth of myth the two basic ingredients of all creation.

When we stop for a few minutes in our gardening activity, we can remember how through it we are connecting with God's creation, celebrating the pleasure and the sustenance the garden gives us, rejoicing in the care and service we can give in return.

Then we take a few more minutes to look inward, listening to these messages from the garden and its tasks for our spiritual lives. It is not hard to draw parallels. We dig and plant our soul's garden in the earlier stages of its cultivation: then we watch the plants grow, whether for beauty or utility. We water and weed them, rejoicing when they prosper and caring for them even more when they wilt.

We have to remember that this spiritual caring also involves the spiritual counterpart of the often painful process of pruning. In the garden, as we cut back the green growth and spreading blossoms, it seems almost a sacrilege. But as gardeners we know it is essential for the future wellbeing of the plants. With this parallel in mind, we will listen to another gardener, speaking in our own day:

> It is more than to be regretted, it is tragic, that we seem to have lost the insight that growth in Christ requires careful pruning. Pieces of us by our intentional action need to die if we are to become the person that is in God's vision. We are not cutting away a cancerous growth, but making room for intended growth.[33]

When we next have to make a resolution, whether to give up something or take up something, this idea of pruning for better growth can be especially helpful.

But for now, to conclude and to take us on into meditation, we return to the light-hearted mood with which we began with Thomas Tusser. It is true, that these verses by Kipling can be read in a similar mood but as with Tusser's directions, Kipling's celebration of the gardener's toil can offer us an underlying message. His 'Glory of the Garden' can become nothing less than a celebration of our sharing, as gardeners, in the continuing, hard, and unremitting work of God in his creation:

Our England is a garden, and such gardens
                                        are not made
By singing: — 'Oh, how beautiful!' and sitting
                                        in the shade,
While better men than we go out and start
                                        their working lives
At grubbing weeds from gravel-paths with
                                        broken dinner-knives.

There's not a pair of legs so thin, there's not
                                        a head so thick,
there's not a hand so weak and white, nor yet
                                        a heart so sick,
But it cannot find some needful job that's crying
                                        to be done,
For the Glory of the Garden glorifieth every one.

Then seek your job with thankfulness and
                                        work till further orders,
If its only netting strawberries or killing slugs
                                        on borders;
And when your back stops aching and your
                                        hands begin to harden,
You will find yourself a partner in the
                                        Glory of the Garden.

Oh, Adam was a gardener, and God
                              who made him sees
That half a proper gardener's work is done
                              upon his knees,
so when your work is finished, you can wash
                              your hands and pray
For the Glory of the Garden, that it may
                              not pass away!
And the Glory of the Garden it shall never pass away![34]

— 9 —

AT REST IN THE GARDEN

My choice for the start of our theme of 'Rest in the Garden' will become clear when we reflect on it further. It is the well-known poem by W.B.Yeats, 'The Lake Isle of Innisfree':

> I will arise and go now and go to Innisfree,
> And a small cabin build there, of clay and
> > wattles made:
> Nine bean rows will I plant there, a hive for
> > the honey bee,
> And live alone in the bee-loud glade.
>
> And I shall have some peace there, for peace
> > comes dropping slow,
> Dropping from the veils of the morning to
> > where the cricket sings;
> There midnight's all a glimmer, and noon
> > a purple glow,
> And evening full of linet's wings.
>
> I will arise and go now, for always night and day
> I hear lake water lapping with low sounds
> > by the shore;
> While I stand on the roadway, or
> > on the pavements grey,
> I hear it in the deep heart's core.[35]

I chose these lines because they seem to me to express a universal human longing for a sanctuary of peace amid the noise and demands of our everyday lives. We may know we will never actually arrive at our equivalent of Yeat's 'lake isle' but we still yearn for it. Nor are we merely seeking an escape from responsibilities. This is a profoundly genuine need in our lives and we should listen to it 'in the deep heart's core'.

That is what we are going to do as we begin to reflect on how far a Quiet Garden can fulfil the need. I like to think that Yeats' sanctuary is indeed a garden, with its nine bean rows and its beehive. But his ideal garden sanctuary is probably well beyond the limits of our aspirations — until we look at them from another perspective and begin to realise that they can be met even without leaving the 'pavements grey' and within earshot of the city roadway. In their book *The Sanctuary Garden* Christopher and Tricia McDowell tell us how we need travel no further than our own front porch to find our island of peace:

> If you create a Sanctuary Garden in your life, remember why you are doing so. It has something to do with nurturing peace within and without, with fostering a relationship in a special place, even if it is simply a chair sitting in your porch or balcony with a few potted plants. Let that be your Sanctuary Garden. The purity of your devotion and intention is what matters . . .

We have to find a way to balance the demands made on us on the one hand by our families, friends, work, and on the other by our personal needs for re-creation and refreshment. And these needs are primarily spiritual ones, even if we don't always recognise them as such and they appear more as physical demands for time and rest. Here are the McDowell's again:

> Our worldly activities, whether we realise it or not, must find balance with the sacred or spiritual. . . . A special setting, and especially one we have created

ourselves, always seems to give us permission to take the time and space to be in it. In a sacred space like a Sanctuary Garden, we come back into owning our time — and, thus, owning ourselves.[36]

I would prefer to continue this process by an offering of our retrieved time and recollected selves to God, for him to return the offering, completed by his blessing.

It is true that time can seem to stand still in a garden, or at least to move more slowly. We still prefer a sundial in a garden as a more appropriate measure of time than a clock. Our gardening activities are fulfilled in our resting, our enjoyment of the fruits of our labour. And we must not forget that our physical renewal through rest is an essential preparation for renewal of the spirit. It would be a sad situation it we were so busy with the activity that we failed to allow time for the resting. After all, we have the greatest example of all when we are told that God walked at evening in the Garden of Eden, the time for relaxation and refreshment.

To deepen this mood of garden-quiet I am adding two stanzas from Andrew Marvell's poem 'The Garden':

Fair quiet, have I found thee here,
And Innocence thy Sister dear!
Mistaken long, I sought you then
In busie Companies of Men.
Your sacred Plants, if here below,
Only among the Plants will gow.
Society is all but rude,
To this delicious Solitude.

. . .

Mean while the Mind, from pleasure less,
Withdraws into its happiness:
The Mind, that ocean where each kind
Does straight its own resemblance find;

Yet it creates, transcending these,
Far other Worlds, and other seas;
Annihilating all that's made
To a green Thought in a green Shade.[37]

Marvell was involved in the political life of the country at the time of Cromwell and then the Restoration, a man very much at the centre of public life for whom the garden was a much valued retreat. His lines here can be read in different ways but it is the overall mood to which we respond and which has made the poem as a whole so much loved. We feel we enter a green world where all is quiet and as we do so, the mind likewise retreats into itself, quiet and responsive to the reflections and daydreams that seem part of the scene.

Such daydreams are often the gateway to a deeper awareness of another dimension to our world. Provided we pass on from this mood to one of attention to God's presence, we will find the stillness, the 'green thought in a green shade', has turned inward to create a Quiet Garden where dreams and thoughts are now transformed into prayer.

— 10 —

THE GARDEN OF THE GOSPELS:
A MEDITATION FOR HOLY WEEK AND EASTER

There is surely a profound significance in the place occupied by the garden in the Gospel narrative. Christ's Passion began in the Garden of Gethsemane and concluded in the Garden of the Burial — which on Easter morning is transformed into the Garden of the Resurrection.

There is a long tradition where these Gardens of the Gospels have been compared and contrasted with the Garden of Eden. In the Garden of Eden death entered human life. In the Gardens of the Passion and Resurrection, Christ overcame human death, bestowing also the divine life of the soul. This association has been present in the Prayer of the Church from very early days, clearly expressed in the following extract from an anonymous ancient homily:

> For your sake , for the sake of man, I became like a man without help . . . For the sake of you, who left a garden, I was betrayed to the Jews in a garden, and I was crucified in a garden. See on my face the spittle I received in order to restore to you the life I once breathed into you. See there the marks of the blows I received in order to refashion your warped nature to my image. On my back see the marks of the scourging I endured to remove the burden of sin that weighs upon your back. See my hands, nailed firmly to a tree, for you who once wickedly stretched out your hand to a tree.
>
> I slept on the cross and a sword pierced my side for you who slept in Paradise . . . My sleep will rouse you

51

from your sleep in hell. The sword that pierced me has sheathed the sword that was turned against you. . . . The enemy led you out of the earthly paradise. I will not restore you to that paradise, but I will enthrone you in heaven. I forbade you the tree that was only a symbol of life, but see, I who am life itself am now one with you.[38]

It doesn't matter whether we believe in the actual earthly paradise and the story of Adam and Eve. We believe in the truth it communicates: that humanity was created to live in harmony with the Creator and his creation, for which the garden remains the most compelling symbol as the place where divine, natural and human life can still work together.

Likewise, we know that at some point it all went wrong and human life broke away from that harmony to seek its own ends, bringing pain and death. The harmony was again made possible when God became man and by his acceptance, overcame death as the effect of the Fall.

So the anonymous writer of the lines I quoted was taking up a very profound truth in the Gospel narrative. The Garden of Eden becomes the Garden of Gethsemane as Christ in his agony undergoes our human fear in the face of the pain and death that destroyed the original harmony represented by that first Garden. In this Garden, his obedience overcomes the original disobedience.

From here I think we can follow the Passion with the same idea in mind. We are told that 'near to the place' of his death there was a garden. Christ from the cross could see a garden that must have represented for him then the destruction of the harmony he came to restore. And when he was buried in that garden tomb, the Garden of Death was transformed, on Easter day, to the Garden of Life. Only, as the writer of the homily reminds us, it is not to the harmony of a restored earthly paradise that could again be destroyed. Instead it is to the promise of an eternal harmony in the new heaven and the new earth.

During Lent, therefore, the garden can become a very special source for meditation and so, for prayer. We can, perhaps, reflect on our soul as a garden. First, a garden of Eden where we face our human limitations and failures. Then, as the Garden of Gethsemane where we watch with Christ and learn from him how to accept and so overcome the doubts and fears that result from our limitations and failures. As we then follow him through his Passion to the Resurrection, our garden of the soul passes from its winter darkness to the springtime of Easter. Furthermore, our actual gardens have followed a similar process, lying fallow through the dark months of Lent and gradually being transformed into the spring green of Easter.

Here I find there is a special place in our meditations for Mary Magdalen. She was the one chosen by Christ to be the first to encounter him in the Garden and the first to carry the Resurrection Message to his other followers. She was chosen, I think we can say, because she had known the depths of degradation and shame, enduring a Gethsemane of pain before her earlier encounter with Christ and its transformation through her self-giving love. Perhaps we can think of her as a special patroness of gardens and, even more, of the Quiet Gardens with their message of re-creative life.

To enter our time for meditation, Mary Magdalen is the subject of this Easter poem by Mary Coleridge:

When Mary thro' the garden went
      There was no sound of any bird,
And yet, because the night was spent,
      The little grasses lightly stirred,
      The flowers awoke, the lines heard.

When Mary thro' the garden went,
      The dew lay still on flower and grass,
The waving palms above her sent
      Their fragrance out as she did pass,
      No light upon the branches was.

When Mary thro' the garden went,
      Her eyes, for weeping long, were dim,
The grass beneath her footsteps bent,
      The solemn lilies, white and slim,
      These also stood and wept for him.

When Mary thro' the garden went,
      She sought, within the garden ground,
One for whom her heart was rent,
      One who for her sake was bound,
      One who sought and she was found.[39]

— 11 —

ANGELS IN THE GARDEN

Our Quiet Gardens vary widely in their outward characteristics but they have certain features in common. In a Quiet Garden we experience what is rare these days: how inseparable is the interplay between our spiritual and physical life.

If we apply this truth about our gardens to our reflections on the Angels, it reminds us how we are so used to thinking of Angels in terms of white robes and wings that it can be quite difficult to realise that those who have encountered them seldom realise they have done so until later. This is, I think, partly because today we are so far separated from the spiritual dimension of our lives. In the Bible, Angels may be recognised as such but usually not primarily by any outward appearance. Usually, they are recognised in the first instance by the inward eye, the vision that Francis Thompson says we now lack:

> The Angels keep their ancient places:—
> Turn but a stone and start a wing!
> 'Tis we, 'tis our estranged faces
> That miss the many-splendoured thing.[40]

We will return to Thompson's poem later but at first we could not do better than reflect on the Angels as they speak to us and come to us through the words and events of the Old and New Testaments.

The first mention of an Angel in the Bible is the 'Angel with a fiery sword' placed at the entrance to the Garden of Eden after the departure of Adam and Eve.

55

It is, at first thought, a negative role. But we need to understand the whole story as myth and with the validity of myth rather than of history. Then the Garden becomes the setting of our first innocence, to which we cannot return but is yet guarded for us by an Angel - our Guardian Angel. This Angel has no fiery sword but is our guide to that place of ultimate happiness for which we believe we were created and which the Garden also represents.

There seems no doubt that it was an Angel who intercepted Abraham when he carried out the command from God, to kill the son whose birth was so full of promise of a great future. Abraham's faith is such that we find it hard to comprehend, as hard as he must have found it to sustain. The Angel came as a messenger to him with a promise repeating an earlier one, that 'all nations on earth will bless themselves by your descendants, because you have obeyed my command.' But how much did the boy Isaac himself understand of all this? We are not told, but for him this Angel was certainly an Angel Guardian.[41]

In Jacob's dream the Angels are passing up and down the ladder reaching between heaven and earth. They are the link between earth and heaven as the promise to Abraham is repeated, that in his grandson 'all clans on earth will bless themselves by you and your descendants'.[42]

It has always been assumed that the stranger with whom Jacob wrestled all night was an Angel. It is a mysterious story, perhaps with the purpose of showing how Jacob had to accept his human limitations as a condition for accepting his place in the history of redemption. If so, his permanent limp that was the outcome of the struggle would be the constant reminder.[43]

The story of Tobias and the Angel has many messages for us and is unfairly neglected. But the one that stands out in connection with the Angel is the interplay between the supernatural world and the human and natural one. The Angel Raphael appears as 'Azarias' to Tobit, describing himself as 'a brother Israelite'. He is, he says, well qualified to accompany Tobit's son, Tobias, on the journey to their kinsman in Medea since he knows the route from long experience. Yet we know he is qualified to act as a guardian for a very different reason and the subsequent story confirms how close we are to supernatural protection provided we get our priorities right.[44]

The growing association between Angels and guardianship and protection is clear in the later story of the three youths thrown into the furnace when they refused to worship King Nebuchadnezzar as a god. The king cries out in astonishment that he sees a fourth man walking with them in the midst of the fire, all four unharmed and the fourth 'like a child of the gods' whom he later describes as 'an Angel'.[45]

In the New Testament the Angels surrounding the birth of Christ serve to draw the two worlds together even more clearly in their twofold role as messengers and guardians. The Angel Gabriel comes as a messenger to Zachariah and then to Mary. In his appearances to Saint Joseph he comes as the guardian, first protecting Mary from Joseph's doubts and then protecting them both with the Child from the wrath of Herod and finally guiding Joseph to their home in Nazareth.

The Angels at the birth of Christ are again messengers to the shepherds. Less well remembered are the Guardian Angels who ministered to Christ after his temptation in the desert. As man, his own Guardian angel came to strengthen him in the Garden of Geth-semane before his Passion and there are then the angelic messengers in the Garden of the Resurrection.

Angels came to comfort the Apostles at the Ascension and it was Peter's Guardian Angel who delivered him from prison.

An Angel was the bearer of one of the most vital messages to the early Church when one appeared to the gentile Cornelius and directed him to send for Peter, resulting in the opening of the Church to the whole gentile world.

By taking these references together we find how distinct the role of the Angels becomes throughout the Bible. They are at once messengers linking human and divine life and they are guardians of our human life in our journey to our home in heaven. Perhaps from here we can meditate on how the angels have continued their twofold role since and even in our own lives. We may not see or hear them but we can be very much aware of their presence if only we remember, as Francis Thompson says, to 'Turn but a stone and start a wing'.

I would now like to add the first and third verses of the poem:

> O world invisible, we view thee,
> O world intangible, we touch thee,
> O world unknowable, we know thee,
> Inapprehensible, we clutch thee!
>
> Not where the wheeling systems darken,
> And our benumbed conceiving soars!—
> The drift of pinions, would we hearken,
> Beats at our own clay-shuttered doors.

We inhabit a world where the invisible elements are as close to us as the visible, if we only have the capacity to be aware and angels are among the most potent links between our physical and our spiritual selves. To lead on to our meditation we can now think back to the many Biblical examples of this role of the angels in our lives: then see how they underlie Francis Thompson's awareness of their presence in our world today as he, too, draws on the Bible for this final example:

> But (when so sad thou canst not sadder)
> Cry:— and upon thy so sore loss
> Shall shine the traffic of Jacob's ladder
> Pitched betwixt Heaven and Charing Cross.

THE CLOISTER GARDEN

To enter this garden from our own time we need to enter
its historical background. History in this sense is no
hindrance to devotion. In fact I find history can enhance
it when our little contemporary experiences get caught up
in an ongoing process, giving them depth and meaning.
We will return to this idea later after looking back to the
way the cloister garden has evolved since the days of the
first Christian monasteries.

We need to keep in mind the two-fold meaning of
the term 'cloister'. It can refer to the monastery as a
whole as well as to what is technically the 'cloister garth'
or garden. So it often happens that when the early
writers refer to the 'cloister' as a kind of 'paradise' they
are referring to the monastery as a whole and the life led
there. As early as the third century there were religious
foundations in the Eastern desert which, through their
devout way of life, recalled for some observers a Garden
of Eden before the Fall. Even the collection of lives of
the monks was given the title the Book of Paradise:

> Now when evening cometh thou must rise up to hear
> the praises, and the psalms which are sent up to Christ
> by the people from the monasteries which are there,
> and a man might imagine his mind being exalted, that
> he was in the paradise of Eden.[46]

In the West, these influences from the Eastern origins of
monasticism were also directed by the long established
tradition associated with Roman gardens. We know from
the remains of the gardens at Pompeii how the family life

revolved around the central atrium or garden. So when the first monastic families arose, it was natural that they built their houses on the Roman plan with the garden at the centre. Paulinus of Nola founded a community of families rather similar to some of our communes today. Their houses were grouped around the church and to reach it from his own house, Paulinus planted a garden. Here he could walk in peace and prepare for the services and make his thanksgiving afterwards.

This was to become the central role of the cloister as the garden. We need to remember that the life of both religious and laity in the Middle ages was in many ways as overcrowded and noisy as our own — and with much worse smells. So the garden within the monastery became a kind of haven easily thought of as a 'paradise', while the herb garden was similarly associated with cleansing and healing. Equally, to the traveller who often found his only safety in the monastic guesthouse, the monastery itself appeared as a 'paradise'. So the tradition, begun long ago in the East, continued.

In the ninth century the abbey of Cluny in southern France was the greatest of the Benedictine foundations. When Saint Peter Damian came to it after a long journey, he identified the spiritual life led there with the physical refreshment offered to the traveller:

> I saw a Paradise watered by the four streams of the Gospels, overflowing with spiritual virtues. I saw a garden bringing forth all kinds of roses and lilies, heavy with sweet fragrance of scents and spices . . . And what else can I call the monastery of Cluny but a field of the Lord, where such a great company of monks living in charity stands like a harvest of heavenly corn?[47]

The abbey of St Gall in Switzerland was another of the great Benedictine foundations. In the ninth century a plan was drawn up for it that provides us with an authentic record of an ideal monastic foundation. The way of life is represented in the order and harmony of the layout, all centred on the great abbey church. The precise attention to detail is very noticeable in the placing and functions of the gardens. The great cloister garden itself is as usual situated next to the church but the layout contains many others as well. The physic garden includes the names of the herbs grown there, together with roses and lilies. The scents of flowers were regarded as beneficial to the sick as well as the healing herbs. The burial ground is planted with orchard trees, a not infrequent use of cemeteries, and the vegetable garden is distinguished by the words 'here the fair plants grow green and tall'. The flower garden nearby provides flowers for the main church and the novitiate and infirmary chapels. On the plan the gardener has his own house here, with accommodation as well for his tools and other equipment.

At least in respect of its gardens, the ideal does not seem to have been far from the reality at St Gall. The abbey became a special centre for the study of medicine, depending on the exact knowledge of the uses of the medicinal herbs grown in the herb garden Several well-known works were produced at St Gall but the one we are interested in is the first known gardening treatise, dating also from the ninth century and written by one Walafrid Strabo. It begins with a charming verse dedication to his Abbot, Grimald, whose own private garden was also open for the pleasure of the boys from the monastery school:

When under the hedge of your garden you sit
In a bower of leaves by your apple tree made
Reinforced by a peach, inferior shade,
Whilst the boys of your school (happy centre of light)
Amuse themselves gathering up in your sight
The most silvery fruit with the softest of bloom,
And try in the palms of their hands to make room
For the curve of some great swelling apple to hide;
Then dear Father, this poem a text will provide
For your lessons . . .[48]

Of course, within the enclosure life was full of stresses
and conflicts. Human nature does not change with the
tonsure. But there was, and still is, the difference
symbolised by the enclosure and in that sense the
monastic life as an ideal was a kind of 'paradisal garden.'
In particular, to the secular world the life within those
precincts could be compared to a garden of paradise
enclosed and secure from the conflicts and stresses of
contemporary life.

William Langland's long poem 'The Vision of
Piers Plowman' gives us a wonderfully varied record of
medieval England. He expresses this ideal even as he
castigates the lax morals of many of the communities of
his time:

For if hevene be on this erthe and ere to any soule
It is in the cloistre or in scole be many skilles I fynde,
For in cloistre cometh ne man to chide ne to fighte,
But alle is buxomnest there and bokes to rede and to
lerne.[49]

When the Cistercians and Carthusians broke away from
the mainstream of the Benedictine Order it was to return
to a more simple and primitive interpretation of the Rule.
For them the life within the enclosure was therefore often

63

identified with the simplicity and beauty of the actual gardens. The Carthusians aimed at restoring the hermit's way of life with each member of the community living in his little 'hermitage' surrounding the central Church. Each had his own garden for flowers and vegetables; a model to contribute, seven hundred years later, to the Garden City movement.

The friars led a very different life and often within cities rather than places of great natural beauty such as those deliberately chosen by the older orders. But we all know of Saint Francis's love of the natural world and its beauties, to become a characteristic of his Order as a whole. He himself had a special love of the garden as representing God's presence in his creation. In their poverty the Friars tended to use their gardens for vegetables but Thomas of Celano recorded in the second of his two *Lives* of the Saint:

> He bade the gardener not dig up the outlying parts of the garden, in order that in their seasons the greenness of grass and beauty of flowers might proclaim the beauteous Father of all things. In the garden he ordered a plot to be set aside for sweet scented and flowering plants, that they might cause those that should look on them to remember the Eternal Sweetness.[50]

Now we will return to our own day, after centuries when the religious Orders lost their central place in the life of the secular world. Today, despite the decline in their numbers and many changes in outlook and custom, their importance is again being recognised. The need for periods of quiet and spiritual and physical renewal is greater now than it ever was and it is being met by the religious Orders, whether the old established ones or the newer foundations. And their gardens form an essential part of the 're-creation' they provide. The cloister garden, in whichever way we regard it, is no longer only a subject for historical study. Its revival represents the revival of a way of life which is again entering our secular world, however differently expressed in outward manner and custom.

Can we see our Quiet Gardens as forming a part of this revival? When we join with others to spend a few hours together in prayer and re-creation, physical as well as spiritual, we are carrying on the tradition that inspired Aelred of Riveaux when he wrote of his community:

> . . . As I was walking round the cloisters, all the brethren sat together, grouped like a most lovely garland. And I gazed on them, as Adam must have gazed on the leaves and the trees and flowers and fruits amidst the delights of Paradise . . . And I was filled with such great joy that it surpassed any delight that this world could give . . .[51]

— 13 —

MEMORIES IN THE GARDEN

These simple lines describing a remembered garden help
to create a mood where we will listen to the voice of our
own memories calling from gardens of the past:

> There is a grey-walled garden far away
>> From noise and smoke of cities where the hours
>> Pass with soft wings among the happy flowers
> And lovely leisure blossoms every day.

> There, tall and white, the sceptral lily blows;
>> There grow the pansy, pink and columbine,
>> Brave hollyhocks and star-white jessamine
> And the red glory of the royal rose.

> There greeny glow-worms gem the dusky lawn,
>> The lime-trees breathe their fragrance to the night,
>> Pink roses sleep, and dream that they are white
> Until they wake to colour with the dawn.

> There in the splendour of the sultry noon
>> The sunshine sleeps upon the garden bed,
>> Where the white poppy droops a drowsy head
> And dreams of kisses from the white full moon.

> And there, all day, my heart goes wandering
>> Because there first my heart began to know
>> The glories of the summer and the snow,
> The loveliness of harvest and of spring.

> There may be fairer gardens — but I know
>> There is no other garden half so dear
>> Because 'tis there, this many, many a year,
> The sacred sweet white flowers of memory grow.[52]

I know myself that among my own childhood memories the best ones are nearly all linked in some way with a garden. That seems to be true for most of us who in our adult years have a special love for gardens and their meaning. The soil was prepared very early and the seeds sown.

Garden memories being so often associated with childhood they also often arouse a nostalgia for a past we know has gone for ever. The nostalgia and the most likely reason for it have been well expressed by Michael Mayne in his writing for his grandchildren:

> It seems to be part of the gut-feeling of being human to experience a sense of yearning, even of loss, a restless, seeking spirit which can feel like a kind of homesickness. There are times when we ache for that which will fulfil and complete us; a longing, it may be, for the lost state of innocence, the Eden of our childhood, or for a future when all questions are answered and we are home at last.[53]

Such nostalgia, at times inseparable from yearning for an unknown future, can be identified with memories arising from a level defined by C.G.Jung as the 'collective unconscious'. At this level we are in touch with the mythical origins of our Western heritage, aware that we were created to be happy and to live in a world of harmony and peace.

So we look back to childhood as the closest we can ever be to that state, even if it is only through our adult eyes that we see childhood in this relation to our later years. Paradoxically, as children our very innocence means we are unable to recognise it.

Not that they need to be nostalgically sad. Some

of the most convincing and beautiful of such memories
are recalled by the seventeenth-century mystic and poet
Thomas Traherne:

> Certainly Adam in Paradise had not more sweet and
> curious apprehensions of the world than when I was a
> child.
> All appeared new, and strange at first, inexpressibly
> rare and beautiful . . . I seemed as one brought into
> the Estate of Innocence. All things were spotless and
> pure and glorious . . . I knew nothing of sickness or
> death or rents or exaction, either for tribute or for
> bread. In the absence of these I was entertained like
> an Angel with the works of God in their splendour and
> glory, I saw all in the peace of Eden; Heaven and
> Earth did sing my Creator's praises, and could not
> make more melody to Adam than to me. All Time was
> eternity, and a perpetual Sabbath.[54]

By the time he recalled these memories Traherne had
travelled a long way towards that union with the unseen
world which spans time, leaving nostalgia behind in its
awareness of God as eternally present throughout the
course of our lives. We can aim for a similar union but
no doubt for most of us our memories from childhood
will be tinged with some sadness, with some regrets, even
occasionally with remorse for what may lie between now
and then. But whereas such memories are precious,
bringing sweetness with the sadness, remorse is always
sour, negative. It betrays our failure to respond to the
most important remembrance of all, that of the loving
forgiveness of God throughout our lives. Regrets are
likewise negative. 'What might have been' may form an
inevitable part of the memories of most of us, what could
have followed the childhood garden and did not. But
they have to be contained within the bounds of a

68

nostalgia that does not disturb an otherwise precious memory and can even enhance it.

Memory is inseparable from the passage of time, as poets and lovers have constantly assured us. It is for us to respond to our own remembered past according to our life-experience. For each it will be different but there is one unifying element for those of us who believe in a God who transcends time. Whatever the sweetness or the sadness, the resulting nostalgia or even regret, the memories are held in the hand of God — where we can leave them safely to rest.

Beyond our individual memories there is the mysterious, deeper memory reaching back to a kind of universal childhood in which we sense we have all partaken . For Jung it is part of our collective unconscious but it is equally known to the mystic and the poet, beautifully explored by T.S.Eliot in his poem 'Burnt Norton'. He passes from a past of 'what might have been' to memories leading on to a present where the remembered garden with its sweetness and its sadness becomes his central image:

> What might have been and what has been
> Point to one end, which is always present.
> Footfalls echo in the memory
> Down the passage we did not take
> Towards the door we never opened
> Into the rose-garden. My words echo
> Thus, in your mind.
> > But to what purpose
> Disturbing the dust on a bowl of rose-leaves
> I do not know.
> > Other echoes
> Inhabit the garden. Shall we follow?

Quick, said the bird, find them, find them,
Round the corner. Through the first gate,
Into our first world, shall we follow
The deception of the thrush? into our first world.

For we cannot live in a remembered world. Memory has to serve the present or it could bury present and future in a fruitless past. So Eliot concludes this passage in the poem with lines that serve well to lead on to our meditation:

Go, said the bird, for the leaves were full of children,
Hidden excitedly, containing laughter.
Go, go, go, said the bird: human kind
Cannot bear very much reality.
Time past and time future
What might have been and what has been
Point to one end, which is always present.[55]

— 14 —

THE HEALING GARDEN

Our first thought in connection with the theme 'The Healing Garden' is of the herb garden and how it has influenced the history of medicine from antiquity down to the present day. Nor should its influence on cookery and cosmetics be forgotten although our concern here is with its healing associations.

There is probably more use of herbs today than there has been since the Middle Ages. As people turn more and more to natural sources for food and medicine so herbs and herb gardens have begun to be invested with something of the importance attached to them in the past

I make no apology here for including some historical background: history can contribute greatly to our appreciation of God's guiding presence in our world. The use of medicinal herbs was well developed in the ancient world but much of the knowledge was lost in the upheavals following the collapse of the Roman Empire. Only far away in distant Britain there was a virtually independent body of such knowledge which survived into the Saxon period to become unique for the time. Much of it was still based on earlier sources and beliefs in pagan deities with their mystical powers over the processes of the natural world. The monks who inherited this wisdom translated the pagan elements into Christian uses. This prayer of an early pagan herbalist to the Earth Goddess was easily baptised into one addressed to God the Father:

> Hear, I beseech thee, and be favourable to my prayer. Whatsoever herb thy power dost produce, give, I pray, with goodwill to all nations to save them and grant me

this my medicine. Come to me with thy powers, and howsoever I may use them may they have good success and to whomsoever I may give them. Whatever thou dost, grant it may prosper. To thee all things return. Those who rightly receive these herbs from me, do thou make them whole.[56]

The herbals composed during the Old English period and beyond testify to the detailed knowledge of the monks who were the chief authors. They were also often artists and their illustrations can combine artistic ability with scientific accuracy to an extent we might well envy today.

So when we decide to plant a bed of herbs in our gardens we are sustaining a very long tradition where, from the earliest times, science and art have united with religious beliefs to provide healing and health. Here we can also recall that the patron saint of gardens and gardeners, Saint Fiacre, was a noble prince who later entered the monastery at Breuil in France which became famous for the herbs he grew there and for their healing properties. However much we owe to our pagan ancestors, the healing process is central to our Christian heritage, reaching back to Christ's own mission of restoring health to mind and body as an essential accompaniment to the healing of the soul.

Herb gardens are by no means the only gardens associated with healing. For the past two centuries the allotment garden has provided nourishment that is not limited to its vegetables and fruit. Countless workers have found an oasis of peace even in the most industrialised districts and the struggle to retain them continues. There were similar city gardens for the poor of London as far back as the twelfth century but we associate the allotment garden more especially with the spread of industry and the bleak deprived life it brought about. The allotment could bring something of the lost countryside into that life, described poignantly in these lines from Peter Walton's poem 'The Allotment':

> . . . Not merely
> that there were a hundred plots or so, but all
> The ways in which it had become a rooted place.
> Sixty years of growth had changed the access tracks
> To country lanes, with chest-high privet
> Rose-and-bramble-trimmed secluding favoured plots.
> A stranger looking at them, I thought
> Of cottage gardens without cottages:
> All else was there — in dilapidated sheds;
> A pigeon loft (against the rules perhaps);
> The old pot, gnome, and weather-vane; and rows
> And rows of vegetables, green enfilades
> Against the surrounding town, miraculously
> Stopped short there . . .[57]

We think of the allotment gardener as essentially a rather lonely figure, preferring perhaps his own company as a release from the crowded life of work and home. There is still a vital place for such gardens in our cities but today there is another city garden making an increasing impact on urban life throughout the industrialised world. Community gardens combine many of the features of the allotment but of their nature they are communal, offering mutual support and companionship in a garden setting where, as with the allotment, the growing of its produce is only one aspect of its restorative properties. Here we will listen to Father Jim O'Donell describing how his garden in one of the poorest districts of Cleveland, Ohio, became a place of physical and spiritual healing:

> The corner where we have that park called 'Oasis of Peace' was filled with rocks and glass and junk. Some-

73

how it reflected the neighbourhood, and it reflected how people felt. In my own heart I'm thinking, let's turn that corner into a garden of love. Let's put flowers and plants and trees in there, so that people see one pocket, one little place that says it's beautiful, and everything isn't junk down here, and we're not all junk — we're not all to be thrown away.

There were so many older men at that time that hung out down at the park. . . . They were all alcoholics. They were people who'd spent anywhere from ten to twenty years in prison and just were down in life, just didn't find much meaning in their life. My way of becoming one with them one day was to go up there - they were all drinking their beer or their wine out of their brown paper bags, and they knew I didn't drink. So one guy bought me a coke and put it in a brown paper bag and said, 'Here you are, rev baby.' So I drank that day with them. It was great. That garden became a place where I, at least for a while, could take the bottle out of one hand and put the shovel in the other hand. And that was a wonderful gift.

I found that a lot of these men were especially gifted. Some of them had been construction workers, some had been carpenters, and some of them had been really good labourers. When I would go to do things, they'd tell me that's not the way you do it! And it wasn't, and I didn't know! I thought, great, you show me, I just want you here . . .

So there's always somebody trying to make it a little bit better. The whole idea was to make people feel that they're good. People *are* good. As one man said, 'I really thought that I was nothing, but when I see people like you and Sister Maggie come down here, I feel God must have sent you to tell me I'm a good person'. I said, 'That's right. That's the only reason we're here'.

So that's how we began, and this has evolved over the years. I didn't know a thing about gardening, you know. I never gardened in my life.[58]

It is a long extract but central to our theme. There is so much to meditate here that we hardly need more. But we will conclude by listening to a very different voice with what is in essence a very similar message. Hildegard of Bingen speaks to us from her twelfth-century Benedictine abbey yet her message is as contemporary as Father O'Donell's. Her knowledge of herbs and their medicinal uses was second to none in her time but it is her poet's voice that speaks to us here as she translates their physical blessings to the spiritual level of divine comfort. The words in her poem are spoken by 'Mercy' and they embrace just the response to human frailty that resulted in Father O'Donell's 'garden of love':

Every creature yearns for a loving embrace.
The plants give off the fragrance of their flowers.
The precious stones reflect their brilliance to others.
. . .

I am a soothing herb. I dwell in the dew and in the air
and in all greenness.

My heart fills to overflowing and I give help to others.
I was there when the first words resounded:
'Let there be'.

With a loving eye, I observe the demands of life and feel
myself part of it all.

I lift the broken-hearted and lead them to wholeness.
I am balm for every pain, and my words ring true.[59]

— 15 —

THE WONDER OF THE GARDEN

In a garden we are in touch with a special kind of wonder — far from the great and glorious wonders of the natural world and yet not unaware of them. The simple daisy is made more wonderful when we look up to the tree tops and skies beyond, remembering how the same life is sustaining the minutiae of nature and the mysteries of outer space.

No doubt many of us are familiar with William Blake's response to this kind of wonder:

> To see a World in a Grain of Sand
> And a Heaven in a Wild Flower,
> Hold Infinity in the palm of your hand
> And Eternity in an hour.[60]

It is the same response that we find in these lines by Rainer Maria Rilke, helping to direct our reflections on the wonder we find in a garden setting:

> I find you, Lord, in all things and in all
> my fellow creatures, pulsing with your life;
> as a tiny seed you sleep in what is small
> and in the vast you vastly yield yourself.
>
> The wondrous game that power plays with things
> is to move in such submission through the world:
> groping in roots and growing thick in trunks
> and in treetops like rising from the dead.[61]

As children we take the sense of wonder for granted. Only later we look back and realise what we then possessed and now too often miss. It was part of our childhood innocence of outlook, uncomplicated by any attempt at understanding or self-analysis. On this aspect of our theme there is a simple but profound dialogue in Antoine de Saint-Exupéry's *The Little Prince:*

> 'The men where you live cultivate five thousand roses in one garden and they do not find what they seek!' 'That is true', I said. 'And yet what they are seeking may be found in a single rose or a drop of water'. 'So it can' I answered. And the Little Prince went on 'But the eyes are blind: one must look with the heart'.[62]

I think Jesus was 'looking with the heart' when he rejoiced at the wonder of the field lilies, more glorious than the splendour of the greatest of earth's kings. He never lost that quality of the child's innocence in responding directly to the world around him. Yet we can still 'look with the heart' and regain something of the early wonder, even if now it has to be with a conscious effort. Usually it is a fleeting experience, such as this moment captured by Rosemary Sutcliffe:

> The high-walled garden . . . was flickering with the coloured flame points of crocuses, white and purple and lilac and gold; each crocus opening to the sunlight seemed to me at once a star and a grail; a cup brimming with light. It is one of the Mysteries, surely, this sense of light shining through rather than on, the whole world becomes faintly translucent and the sight of the spirit shining through its substance. . . . One has it as a child, but in childhood one knows nothing else and so is not conscious of it, till the heightened aware-ness is given back for this one time.[63]

For some of us there can be more than one such experience but they are always rare — as they would have to be to sustain the element of wonder. They are usually associated with joy and the release, however fleetingly, from the cares of everyday life. But they can also come as moments of consolation in sorrow, a sudden realisation that, however deep the grief, it will pass and the goodness and beauty of creation around us will remain, a constant wonder with every opening flower.

In a poem called 'The Bright Field', R.S.Thomas has recalled a similar experience where the fleeting moment remains in the memory of a lifetime and beyond:

> I have seen the sun break through
> to illuminate a small field
> for a while, and gone my way
> and forgotten it. But that was the pearl
> of great price, the one field that had
> the treasure in it. I realize now
> that I must give all I have
> to possess it. Life is not hurrying
>
> on to a receding future, nor hankering after
> an imagined past. It is the turning
> aside like Moses to the miracle
> of the lit bush, to a brightness
> that seemed as transitory as your youth
> once, but is the eternity that awaits you.[64]

This is also the special wonder of the garden. It is always there, the pearl awaiting the finding whatever our mood or circumstance. And because we have had a share in creating the garden setting we have an equally special sense of participation in the wonder.

Of its very nature, wonder lies beyond the definition of words. We can only try to describe our own response to an experience that eludes rational understanding or expression. This is the reason I have relied more than elsewhere on recollections and descriptions of such experiences from others. So now to lead on into meditation there are some lines by Francis Thompson which seem to come as close as any to expressing the essence of the kind of wonder we may encounter in the garden:

> This is the enchantment, this the exultation,
> The all-compensating wonder,
> Giving to common things wild kindred
> With the gold-tesserate floors of Jove;
> Linking such heights and such humilities
> Hand in hand in ordinal dances,
> That I do think my tread,
> Stirring the blossoms in the meadow-grass,
> Flickers the unwithering stars.[65]

PART II

by Philip Jebb

— 16 —

MEDITATIONS IN A GARDEN

These notes are intended as a help to meditation, contemplation, in a Quiet Garden. They consist of a series of headings relating to a theme which may assist the heart and mind in communicating with God our Father, Redeemer, Inspirer.

When Jesus was asked by his followers to help them to pray I do not believe he gave them fewer than seventy words to be recited straight through in less than half a minute. I see the clauses of the *Our Father* as separate headings to help raise our heart and mind to God and to receive strong messages from him.

Prayer is a two-way process and we need to receive from God much more than we can offer to him.

So, I am to pray to *our* Father, not just to *mine*: we are all children of the same creator, the whole human race makes up one family, with God our parent, shining out with the qualities of Mother as well as Father; all creation derives from God's creative generation; all our inspiration, work, achievement, energy is dependent upon God's; without God's sustaining power we cease to exist.

This Father (Mother) of ours dwells in Heaven: a state, rather than a place; a state of total and unthreatened bliss, peace, wonder; this is God's settled state and we are created to inherit it forever; all joy and glory derive from this state; we are given glimpses, hints of its quality in the high moments of our present life; we need

80

to set our hearts upon desire for this; we need to recognise God's holiness and work for its fulfilment in us.

So can we work through the various headings given us by Jesus, getting endless help as we adore, petition, feel sorrow and gratitude. A whole hour, with practice, can be spent on any one of the clauses, especially as we learn not only to pour out our hearts, but even more as we desist from our own thoughts and words, remain still in his presence and so receive *his* thoughts, *his* plans, *his* inspiration, his *life*.

So there now follow here a series of major themes relevant to anyone wishing to pray in a garden. They are not to be seen as rigid formulas to be followed exactly, but as gateways, paths, vistas, to help our heart and mind, our love and understanding, to rest and grow in the presence of God in a garden, which was the context in which our first parents had that primeval experience of walking with their creator. Some of them may not be helpful to a particular individual, so skip them; with others it may be possible and desirable to remain praying for several minutes or even for the rest of the time allotted for prayer: work through them with the freedom of the Spirit. Let us hope that some of the thoughts may lead you to create others of your own.

They are not to be seen simply as an intellectual exercise, but rather as a means to love, peace, joy, aids to life in the Spirit. And do not be surprised or put out if the same element appears under different headings: all creation is inter-related, and God is not ashamed to repeat the glory of the dawn, the marvel of dew upon the grass, the sound of wind among the leaves, the scent of violets. Being set in a garden we have but to bring back our wandering attention to what is all around us to have our prayer renewed whenever it seems to falter.

WINTER

Dear Lord, in the Winter you give powerful images
                of both life and death.
You show us with stark insistence the possibility
                of an everlasting rejection of your love,
In images of Hell, the cold, the dark, the dead
                remnants of once vigorous life.
But you have also said that if we are to find
                everlasting life we must go through death.
How urgent is the need for your warmth and light.

        *   *   *   *   *

So at this darkest time, when you were born into
                the world, where do we find Hope and Life?

        *   *   *   *   *

Winter has a message all its own;
But because of the cold we cannot sit and rest:
                we must be on the move to generate
                        warmth within.
But there is beauty and hopeful expectation all
                around us to help us through these harsh days.
The trees are naked, without leaves or flowers or fruit;
But the bare branches give us glimpses of the stars;
They reach their fingers to heaven,
Even as their roots hold fast to the earth,

Linked by the strong trunk, giving interchange of life,
Symbols of our dual nature and inheritance.

At this dark time we find the Moon and stars
                              our friends, closer, more visible,
                                   than at other seasons.
The wind has a different, keener, voice, not muffled
                              by the rustling leaves.
We have the gift of the snow's beauty,
With its purity
And its diamond pinpoints enhancing the
                              poor Sun's feeble rays.
And each flake is a new and unique creation
                         to bring us yet more wonder.
You have not deserted us, dear Lord:
We know that Spring's resurrection is at hand,
Marked by the purple buds already on the branches.
But let us not forget the cold dark, time.
Let us face the significance of death now,
While we are alive and conscious,
And so be ready to pass through its reality
                              in company with you,
Marked with your saving baptism,
To bring us to the glory of new born, everlasting Life.

SPRING

Lord, this is the season of your Resurrection:
There is no accident in its timing:
This rising from the deep sleep of Winter,
With its images of death: the cold and dark,
                    and dead remnants of once vigorous life.
Love is abroad
In our own hearts
In all of Nature.
All living things put on new clothing
                        at your urgent command.
Beauty, *your* Beauty, has returned.
We breathe a new air,
No longer cold with seeming death.
The flowers respond
                    to the strengthening Sun, your light.
So may our hearts respond to your love and grace.
The birds break into song and call us to your praise.
So may our hearts give praise at all aspects of our lives.
The frozen earth and water melt to new life:
So may our hardened hearts be softened
                        to gentleness and love.
We are overwhelmed with images, symbols,
    confirmations, of your resurrecting, your enlivening.
All this is beyond the power of Winter's imagination.
Beauty and Life have returned.
Resurrection is *now*.
Let us choose some Spring flower:
The primrose, the bluebell, the daffodil, the violet,
See its own particular and individual beauty,
Which is your gift:

A brave confirmation of your living, creative power,
And see in this courage, beauty and frail strength
                the symbol of how to pattern our own lives,
With a loving response to your grace,
A generous outpouring of further life
                                into your creation.
Lord, we thank you for the gift of new life.
May we bring it to fulfilment
In ourselves and in those we meet.

— 19 —

SUMMER

Dear Lord, we are at the high tide of the garden's year.
All is at the fullness of the life you give.
There is a new generation of birds and animals,
Nurtured with your loving care, instinct within them.

*   *   *   *   *

The hot Sun and season of Pentecost remind us
        of the Spirit's tongues of flame: warmth and light.
Wind in the leaves gives another symbol of your
        moving Spirit, — all signs of your loving power.

*   *   *   *   *

The Sun is at its strongest and highest in the sky.
With water and soil giving the three elements,
                needed for life in a garden:

Strong image of your creative power,
Calling forth the endless variety of your
                                    creative imagination:
Colour, scent and sound.
Making for Beauty
And for peaceful Joy.

                *   *   *   *   *

Another image of what you are preparing for
                those who, with your inspiration, love you.
You show balance and proportion in your
                                    summer garden:
With the hotter Sun comes more protecting shade
                                    from the trees,
The brighter Sun draws more colour from the flowers;
The bees gather that sunlight as honey
                for their Winter store — and ours,
Even as they help to bring those flowers to fruition,
Symbol of our own often unconscious co-operation
                                    with your plan.
We can touch eternity in a garden:
Let us enjoy it in the present,
Put aside (but be grateful for) all the past
                hard work, our own or others'.
Let us review the gifts and experiences of this day
                in Paradise (the Greek word for a garden).
And now, with open eyes, let us choose some feature
                                    from what surrounds us,
Let us contemplate it, seeing it through your
                                    creative eyes, O Lord
Resting in your creative love.

— 20 —

AUTUMN

Lord God, you walked in a garden at
                    the start of human history.
We can still feel close to you in this place.
The year's work is now coming to fulfilment.
Each of the seasons has its beauty and its gift,
As you speak to us in a garden through all the senses.
You have led us out of the bare elementals
                    and the storms of Winter,
Into the freshness of Spring and the song of the birds.
In the Summer you gave us warmth
                      and luxuriant growth.
The strong light and leaves for shade.

*   *   *   *   *

Now it is the Autumn,
To bring us your stillness, image of eternity.
The leaves are turning to glory,
Rivals of the earlier flowers.
The flowers have turned to seeds and fruit,
For our enjoyment,
Our sustenance,
And our future life.
This is the time of fulfilment and completion.
It has a beauty all its own:
Perfect symbol of your providence.
It makes death less frightening,
As we see the true end of the year,
As we contemplate your loving, overarching plan for us.

We rejoice in the fruits you give us

in your loving generosity.
We look to what *we* can allow *you* to give through us.
We have seen your plan through the first

shoots of Spring,
The flowers and strong growth of Summer,
The fruit of Autumn,
So now let use all our senses to your glory:
Smell the crispness of your air,
Taste your fruit,
See your beauty in the turning leaves,
Rest in your gentle silence,
As we return to the best moment of this day

which you have given us.

— 21 —

EARTH, WATER AND SUN:
IMAGE OF THE TRINITY

Lord God, you revealed to Moses the singleness

of your divine being.
You have no separate name, you are just pure Being:
I AM.
But Jesus revealed the Trinity:
That you are Company,
Not an awesome solitude.
In a garden we find the trinity of

Earth, Water and Sun,
Each essential to maintain the glad reality

of living things.

*   *   *   *   *

The Soil: Humus — whence Humility
Dark and unnoticed,
But the base and foundation of all else,
All life issues from it:
'Mother Earth'
Sustaining Father
First Person of the Trinity.

*   *   *   *   *

Water: powerful image of the Second Person:
Through living water relieving all thirst,

Without water there is no life,
Alive with movement,
Finding its own level,
Transparent, yet reflecting the light.
Washes clean,
Softens the hard earth with rain,
Gives beauty in the morning dew.
Combines two elements, and makes a mysterious third.
Reminds us of our baptism.

*   *   *   *   *

The Sun, image of the Third Person,
'Giver of Life',
Reveals what is hidden.
Brings warmth to the ice-cold earth
And to our frozen hearts.

Brings colour to the earth,
And to our dull hearts,
Enabling us to rejoice in beauty.

*   *   *   *   *

From these three elements, Lord, we obtain
            the endless variety of your creative imagination.
Colour, scent and sound all make for joyous beauty.
In a garden we experience your creative power,
And are allowed to co-operate,
Though it is you who give the increase.

All of this to achieve peaceful *JOY*,
Your settled state,
And to be our secure inheritance:
For all eternity
An image of what you are preparing
                        for those who love you.
How can we do anything but give thanks in a garden?
We can touch eternity in these surroundings:
                  'Time stands still in a garden'.

*   *   *   *   *

Let us open our eyes to be filled with some one aspect
                  of beauty and Joy, your gift.

SEEING IN A GARDEN

Dear Lord, you give me five windows
                   to the world around me:
Sight, hearing, smell, taste and touch.
Each can lead me to some contact, some grasp
                   of your transcendent being.
You, who are the cause, the creator, of both sides
                   of the window.
You who are both within and beyond all creation,
Immanent and transcendent.
Perhaps such awareness is more possible in
                   a garden than anywhere else on earth.
Let me remember that Paradise
                   is the Greek word for a garden.
As I look about me in a garden I see beauty
                   in the colour and pattern of plants,
Each with its own especial nature
                   contributing to the whole:
The stem, the leaf, the bud, the flower, the seed,
Each in its proper place and order;
Each fulfilling a purpose in itself
And beyond itself.
I can see my own self here in relation to you,
Even as the plant relates to the Sun:
With its frailty, and yet its strength;
The beauty of each part and of the ordered whole:
The coming to full flower, to fruition, to decay.
Then to renewal, resurrection, in another year.
I see also the relation of one living thing to another.
I see the infinite variety of your prodigious
                   gift of creation,

Your boundless generosity,
The endless expressions of your love.
For this my eyes were made.
And yet beyond my simple seeing my heart
                              and mind go out to you,
The giver of this gift,
To the transcendent beauty and glory
                    of your own incomprehensible being.

*   *   *   *   *

I see a garden as a resting place,
A place of repose,
And yet of ceaseless activity,
Both images of your divinity.

*   *   *   *   *

I glorify you and give you thanks.

— 23 —

HEARING IN A GARDEN

Dear Lord, how many and marvellous
                           are the gifts you give us
                  through our hearing in a garden.
The chorus of the birds, proclaiming your glory:
The sheer joy and beauty of their song,
The vibrant intensity of their life:
The blackbird and the thrush with their
                           endless variety of song,
And yet to be repeated after
                  'the first sweet careless rapture'.
The defiant challenge of the robin,
The gentle cooing of the dove,
The mournful cawing of the rooks.

               *   *   *   *   *

Beyond and behind that explicit and various chorus,
The insistent, low intensity of the humming insects,
Largely invisible — often almost unnoticed,
Yet awe inspiring in their sheer number
Contributing to the all pervading sound.

               *   *   *   *   *

Besides this, the wind, image of your Spirit,
Breathing gently through the summer leaves,
Or vibrantly sighing when it is strong
                          with Winter's fury.

Great symbol of your love and power,
Invisible, save in the creatures moved by your caress.

* * * * *

Finally, the sound of water:
From the splashing of a fountain,
Rising and falling,
One of your own chosen images of life,
The murmuring of a stream for ever
                              flowing to the boundless sea,
The friendly chatter of a waterfall,
The patter of life-giving raindrops,
Falling from the unreachable sky.

* * * * *

Dear Lord, we thank you for all the images
              and symbols of your greatness and glory
                    that reach us through our ears.

24

SCENT, TASTE AND TOUCH
IN A GARDEN

How evocative of your presence, Lord,
                              is the gift of smell!
The scent of all the different flowers,
Simply to attract and give JOY.
That all pervading, undefined presence,
Image of your divine being, immanent in creation.

*   *   *   *   *

Some gardens are designed for the blind:
Lavender, jasmine, the rose, sweet peas,
Crushed leaves of bay,
And oh, so many more;
The smell of new mown grass,
Of rain quickening the dry earth.
These remind us of your own image
                              of yourself as the gardener.

*   *   *   *   *

We can think first of a garden as the enclosed
                              centre of pleasure,
And so the sweet taste of honeysuckle
                    and all that the bees will gather.
But also we can taste of its fruits:
Apple, cherry and pear,
And all the vegetables to sustain our bodily life,
Besides our hunger and thirst for beauty,

Implanted in us to remind us of our
        everlasting fulfilment to be enjoyed in Paradise,
The heavenly garden.

*   *   *   *   *

Finally, we have the sense of touch
The most fundamental of our senses:
We can feel the warmth of the Summer sun,
The caress of a gentle breeze,
Both images and symbols of love,
Of which you are the origin and source.
We can walk barefoot and feel the soft grass,
The cool dew,
The water of stream or pool,
The hard, smooth paving of a path.
We can receive a message from the living bark of a tree
Handle a stone which has resisted change
                        through a million years,
Smooth or rough — light or heavy:
All gateways to your creative power.

*   *   *   *   *

In all of this we feel your loving touch,
Your promise of eternal contentment.
We thank you, Lord,
As we gently live through all our senses.

25

DIVINE AND HUMAN
CO-OPERATE IN A GARDEN

O Lord,
A garden is the perfect symbol of our working
                             together with you,
Or rather, of your creative love and power
Working through your creatures.
You give the elements of earth and water and sunlight,
Which combined in a garden bring your gift of life.
We have no part in these.
You also give us all our powers and abilities:
The mind to plan,
The strength to prepare the ground,
The patience and faith to wait for the growth,
The ability to enjoy.
In all of these you give us some autonomy.
But we cannot truthfully say 'I grew that rose'.
But perhaps we placed it in the right environment,
In the right relation to other plants,
We encouraged it,
Saved it from threats and rivals,
Gave it fertilizer,
Water when the rain failed,
Pruned it.

*   *   *   *   *

But all these skills and strengths still came from you,
And you gave the increase:
The miraculous growth,

The intricate complexity of every succeeding
stage of the plant.
Likewise your guiding hand and mind
are intimately living in ours:
You *allow* us to exercise this reflection
of your creativity.

*   *   *   *   *

This should teach us humility,
Gratitude,
Wonder:
Humble recognition of what is not ours:
The power and beauty;
Wonder at your power,
The glorious variety of your creative imagination:
Wonder also at your promise that this will
not compare with the glory of the
unending Paradise you are preparing for us;
Gratitude for all your gifts,
Many of which we do not realise,
Or come to slowly:
So much in a garden is hidden:
The interaction of bees
And worms and bacteria
And a myriad other creatures,
All having their part in the intricate web
of its life and growth.
For *all* your gifts,
Known or unrecognised,
And for allowing us to share in them,
We thank you, Lord.

26

PARABLES IN A GARDEN

Dear Lord, so much of your teaching came in parables,
Raising up your hearers from everyday life
                                        to the divine,
Trying to make them at home in both,
Even as you are yourself.
So many of these parables are concerned
                            with living, organic growth,
Perfectly suited to your living creative plan,
Expressions of it so attuned to time in a garden:
The miracle of the mustard seed's growth,
From the smallest of seeds to the largest of shrubs,
Fit for birds to nest in, and so supporting
                                        yet further life:
Model for your Kingdom's growth within us.

*   *   *   *   *

The secret growth of the seed:
First the shoot,
Then the ear,
Then the seed in the ear,
Growing we know not how,
As with all true miracles.

*   *   *   *   *

The cockle weeds amid the corn:
Symbol of our failures
And frustrating sins,
Not to be entirely eradicated until the final judgement.

The seed dying before new life can spring from it:
True pointer, Lord, to your Life, Death —
                              and Resurrection.

*   *   *   *   *

The intimate link between you, the vine,
                        and us the branches:
We can live only in *your* life:
Cut off from your life-giving sap
                we are good for nothing but to be burnt.

*   *   *   *   *

The different forms of failure experienced by the sower,
But the triumph of that which falls on good ground:
May we be found among those bearing a hundredfold.

*   *   *   *   *

The fearful story of the fig tree cursed
                        for its failure to produce its fruit:
Hell is the failure of life,
First here and then hereafter,
Following upon our deliberate choice of self-exclusion
                        from your Divine life
We see the urgent incentive to choose life
                through all the set-backs and labours.

*   *   *   *   *

Your gift of a garden is the perfect setting
                        for receiving your message
And remaining true to it.
We thank you, Lord.

27

EDEN AND GETHSEMANE

Dear Lord,
The story of your dealings with your children
                                  begins and ends in gardens.
Let us remember that Paradise is the Greek word
                                  for a garden,
That primeval home of Joy
Where you set our first parents,
Filled with all delights,
Where you walked with them
In the cool of the evening.
The pictures are clear and beautiful,
And we can recapture them in
                                  our present surroundings.

*   *   *   *   *

But then came the Fall from innocence,
The denial and rejection of your loving friendship,
The exile and desert outside the garden,
So fearfully pictured in the forty years
                                  of the wilderness:
'A dry weary land where no water is'.

*   *   *   *   *

Then, Lord, you returned among us,
Bringing again the Good News of your undying love.
But even so the testing in another garden,
But this time bringing triumph
And everlasting life.

But first your Agony,
As you faced the fearful cost of our Redemption,
Alone, with no support from your friends,
Though at least you were sent an angel
In the place of Eden's serpent.
Then the arrest
And forcible expulsion from the garden,
The trial was in the built up city:
The harsh world of streets and noisy commerce;
The Crucifixion on the bare mount,
Naked as a skull,
Where only the Cross stood for the Tree of Life,
Fearful sign of contradiction.
But then your body, seed of new life,
Was buried in another garden,
Close by that Tree of Life
From which it had been taken.
There did Mary Magdalen find you,
Inspired in mistaking you for the gardener:
For you indeed are the true gardener
And carer of all our destinies.
Here we can find you for evermore:
Every garden can bring us home to you:
We thank you, Lord.

28

TREES IN A GARDEN

How infinitely varied, Lord, are the forms
                                 of life in a garden,
And how interdependent.
Let us consider the City that makes up a tree:
Its own intricate structure;
Roots to gather water and nutriment;
A trunk with the ebb and flow of sap,
Reaching to the uttermost twigs
which sprout from the branches,
Potent symbol of your life-giving grace;
The leaves with individual and characteristic shapes,
As varied and as similar as the individuals
                                 and races of men;
The leaves' flesh, concealing the intricate
                                 skeleton within.
See how this unfolds and grows,
Before the buds can appear to foster the flower,
Itself so wonderfully complex in its delicate beauty,
Pure reminder of Heaven's delight,
Calling the bee by its beauty and its scent,
To delve deep for the sweet store of honey,
And so start the process of fertilising
Which will be consummated in the fruit,
Itself another world of creation:
With seed and flesh and protective skin, shell or pod.
This in its turn returning to the earth,
To start the process of resurrected life,
With the protective coverlet of leaves,
Turned to glory before their sacrificial fall.

*   *   *   *   *

But the tree sustains yet more life:
Birds nesting in its branches
Or its hollow trunk,
Feeding on its fruit,
Sheltering among its leaves.
The insects also, in all their myriad forms,
Inhabiting all the varied aspects of its life;
The earth bound animals sheltering in its shade;
Squirrels, so beautifully adapted to its life.
And when the great giant falls,
There is timber for warmth,
For building,
For furniture,
For sailing the seas.
Lord, how wonderful are your works!

29

THE FAUNA OF A GARDEN

At first glance, dear Lord, the garden consists
                 of plants, in all their myriad forms,
Bearing witness to your creative energy,
Giving you glory by their living growth,
By the pattern of their individual development,
Each of which can be the subject of a lifetime's study,
Food for wonder and gratitude,
Ascending in prayer.
Among these plants there is no free movement,
Only the imperceptible growth on a rooted spot,
Or to be shaken by the passing wind:
Symbol of stability in a single purpose.

*   *   *   *   *

But look again: become aware
              of the other more independent forms of life:
Most obvious, perhaps, the birds,
Feeding — nesting — singing:
Receiving from your riches,
And giving Joy in return.
Then the insects,
From flies to spiders,
Ants to bees,
Occupying all three elements.
The life of pond and stream:
The fish — the frogs and toads — the newts,
The chrysalis, soon to be a dragonfly,
Most potent image of our dual destiny:
First in the murky water,

Slow moving and with little colour or form,
Then darting in the blazing glory of Heaven's light.
Perhaps also the snake,
Gliding over the water,
Or coiled in the Sun,
A thing of beauty if we have the courage to observe it,
But also a reminder of the threats
        and dangers of this life.
Finally the animals that we may meet:
Coming closer to our own form of life,
With warm blood, four limbs and hearts akin to ours.
The squirrels, so delicate in movement
Disdaining the ground,
The scurrying mice, more often heard than seen;
The slow moles, evidenced mostly
      by their little hills erupting on the lawn,
But doing great work to many threats
        beneath the surface;
Perhaps the occasional rabbit, fox or badger,
The deer, so delicate,
And reminding us of the psalm where it yearns
      for running water as we should for grace.
These will come to us if we wait in still silence,
As befits our prayer;
The cats and dogs which are part of our own family,
        and friends indeed.

     * * * * *

Here in our garden is all of life and its wonder,
Leading us to your ultimate glory, Lord,
More than we can hope to encompass
      in our brief lifetime here on earth.
Make us worthy of this tremendous inheritance.

30

LIFE AND DEATH IN A GARDEN

Lord, after your initial gift and inspiration of creation,
Expressing your existence, your essence,
                in limited and varied forms,
Your most amazing gift is *Life*,
Again, in its myriad forms.
And yet each of these forms continues
                       to perpetuate itself.
Here is food for wonder and for thanks.

*   *   *   *   *

But with all these signs of life and growth,
We have around us as many signs of death and decay,
Reminders of our own mortality.
Look at the life of a flower:
Smiling at the Sun for its brief hour;
The attendant leaves, appearing sooner
                      and lasting longer,
But soon answering to the summons of Autumn,
With their gentle return to the earth;
The seeds and fruit issuing from the dead flower,
And falling in their turn.
The plants themselves have their life cycles,
Of birth,
Growth,
Maturity
And death,
Even as we do ourselves.

*   *   *   *   *

But look again at these signs of mortality:
The falling leaves;
The decomposing fruit and seeds,
Together with our pruning and cutting back:
It is only through these little deaths
                that the whole can maintain its greater life:
New vigour from the pruned rose,
Leaves giving compost for the new seeds,
The seeds themselves dying to new life,
As well ordered as day following night,
Or the urgent Spring on the heels
                                of restful, fallow Winter,
Seeming so dead.

*   *   *   *   *

So shall we also find Resurrection and new life
                in your well ordered Paradise.

PART III

SOME CLASSICAL GARDEN POEMS

— 31 —

THE GARDEN

How vainly men themselves amaze,
To win the palm, the oak, or bays,
And their incessant labours see
Crowned from some single herb or tree
Whose short and narrow-vergèd shade
Does prudently their toils upbraid,
While all the flowers and trees do close
To weave the garlands of repose!

Fair quiet, have I found thee here,
And Innocence, thy sister dear?
Mistaken long, I sought you then
In busy companies of men.
Your sacred plants, if here below,
Only among the plants will grow;
Society is all all but rude
To this delicious solitude.

No white nor red was ever seen
So amorous as this lovely green.
Fond lovers, cruel as their flame,
Cut in these trees their mistress' name.
Little, alas! they know or heed,
How far these beauties hers exceed!
Fair trees! wheres'e'er your bark I wound,
No name shall but your own be found.

When we have run our passion's heat,
Love hither makes his best retreat.
The gods, that mortal beauty chase,
Still in a tree did end their race:
Apollo hunted Daphne so,
Only that she might laurel grow;
And Pan did after Syrinx speed,
Not as a nymph, but for a reed.

What wondrous life is this I lead!
Ripe apples drop about my head;
The luscious clusters of the vine
Upon my mouth do crush their wine;
The nectarine, and curious peach,
Into my hands themselves do reach;
Stumbling on melons, as I pass,
Insnared with flowers, I fall on grass.

Meanwhile the mind, from pleasure less,
Withdraws into its happiness;—
The mind, that ocean where each kind
Does straight its own resemblance find;
Yet it creates, transcending these,
Far other worlds, and other seas,
Annihiltating all that's made
To a green thought in a green shade.

Here at the fountain's sliding foot,
Or at some fruit-tree's mossy root,
casting the body's vest aside,
My soul into the boughs does glide:
There, like a bird, it sits and sings,
Then whets and combs its silver wings,
And, till prepared for longer flight,
Waves in its plumes the various light.

Such was that happy garden-state,
While man there walked without a mate:
After a place so pure and sweet,
What other help could yet be meet!
But 'twas beyond a mortal's share
To wander solitary there:
Two paradises 'twere in one,
To live in paradise alone.

How well the skillful gardener drew
Of flowers, and herbs, this dial new;
Where, from above, the milder sun
Does through a fragrant zodiac run,
And, as it works, the industrious bee
Computes its time as well as we!
How could such sweet and wholesome hours
Be reckoned but with herbs and flowers?

Andrew Marvell (1621-1678)

— 32 —

MY GARDEN

A garden is a lovesome thing, God wot!
Rose plot,
Fringed pool,
Ferned grot—
The veriest school
Of peace; and yet the fool
Contends that God is not—
Not God! in gardens! when the eve is cool?
Nay but I have a sign;
'Tis very sure God walks in mine.

Thomas Edward Brown (1830-1897)

THE CHURCH: THE GARDEN OF CHRIST

We are a Garden walled around,
Chosen and made peculiar Ground;
A little Spot enclosed by Grace
Out of the World's wide Wilderness.

Like Trees of Myrrh and Spice we stand,
Planted by God the Father's hand;
And all the Springs in Sion flow,
To make the young Plantation grow.

Awake, O heavenly Wind, and come,
Blow on this Garden of Perfume;
Spirit Divine, descend and breathe
A gracious Gale on Plants beneath.

Make our best Spices flow abroad
To entertain our Saviour-God:
And Faith, and Love, and Joy appear,
And every Grace be active here.

Let my Beloved come, and taste
His pleasant Fruits at his own Feast.
I come, my Spouse, I come, he cries,
With Love and Pleasure in his eyes.

Our Lord into his Garden comes,
Well pleased to smell our poor Perfumes,
And calls us to a Feast Divine,
Sweeter than Honey, Milk, or Wine.

Eat of the tree of Life, my Friends,
The Blessings that my Father sends;
Your taste shall all my Dainties prove,
And drink abundance of my Love.

Jesus, we will frequent thy Board,
And sing the Bounties of our Lord:
But the rich Food on which we live
Demands more Praise than Tongues can give.

Isaac Watts (1674-1748)

— 34 —

PRAISE

For the beauty of the earth,
For the beauty of the skies,
For the love which from our birth
Over and around us lies,
Lord of all, to thee we raise
This our sacrifice of praise.

For the beauty of each hour
Of the day and of the night,
Hill and vale and tree and flower,
Sun and moon and stars of light:
Lord of all, to thee we raise
This our sacrifice of praise.

For the joy of human love,
Brother, sister, parent, child,
Friends on earth, and friends above,
Pleasures pure and undefiled:

Lord of all, to thee we raise
This our sacrifice of praise.

For each perfect gift of thine,
To our race so freely given,
Graces human and divine,
Flowers of earth and buds of heaven:
Lord of all, to thee we raise
This our sacrifice of praise.

For thy church which evermore
Lifteth holy hands above,
Offering up on every shore
Her pure sacrifice of love,
Lord of all, to thee we raise
This our sacrifice of praise

F.S. Pierpoint, (1835-1917)

— 35 —

A WINTER'S TALE

                 . . . Daffodils,
That come before the swallow dares, and take
The winds of March with beauty; violets dim,
But sweeter than the lids of Juno's eyes
Or Cythereas's breath; pale primroses,
That die unmarried ere they can behold
Bright Phoebus in his strength — a malady
Most incident to maids; bold oxlips, and
The crown-imperial; lilies of all kinds,
The flower-de-luce being one!

William Shakespeare (1564-1616)

TO DAFFODILS

Fair daffodils, we weep to see
You haste away so soon;
As yet the early-rising sun
Has not attain'd his noon,
Stay, stay
Until the hasting day
Has run
But to evensong;
And, having pray'd together, we
Will go with you along.
We have short time to stay, as you,
We have as short a spring;
As quick a growth to meet decay,
As you, or anything.
We die
As your hours do, and dry
Away
Like to the summer's rain;
Or as the pearls of morning's dew,
Ne'er to be found again.

Robert Herrick (1591-1674)

KINDLY SPRING

Kindly spring again is here,
Trees and fields in bloom appear;
Hark! the birds with artless lays
Warble their creator's praise.

Where in winter all was snow,
Now the flowers in clusters grow;
And the corn, in green array,
Promises a harvest-day.

Lord, afford a spring to me,
Let me feel like what I see;
Speak, and by thy gracious voice,
Make my drooping soul rejoice.

On thy garden deign to smile,
Raise the plants, enrich the soil;
Soon thy presence will restore
Life to what seemed dead before.

John Newton (1725-1807)

BINSEY POPLARS
felled 1879

My aspens dear, whose airy cages quelled,
Quelled or quenched in leaves the leaping sun,
All felled, felled, are all felled;
    Of a fresh and following folded rank
      Not spared, not one
      That dandled a sandalled
      Shadow that swam or sank
On meadow and river and wind-wandering weed-winding
    bank.

    O if we but knew what we do
      When we delve or hew —
    Hack and rack the growing green!
      Since country is so tender
    To touch, her being só slender,
    That, like this sleek and seeing ball
    But a prick will make no eye at all,
    Where we, even where we mean
      To mend her we end her,
    When we hew or delve:
After-comers cannot guess the beauty been.
    Ten or twelve, only ten or twelve
    Strokes of havoc únselve
      The sweet especial scene,
    Rural scene, a rural scene,
    Sweet especial rural scene.
        Gerard Manley Hopkins (1844-1889)

CONTEMPLATION

This morning saw I, fled the shower,
The earth reclining in a lull of power:
The heavens, pursuing not their path,
Lay stretched out naked after bath,
Or so it seemed; field, water, tree, were still,
Nor was there any purpose
                              on the calm-browed hill.

The hill, which sometimes visibly is
Wrought with unresting energies,
Looked idly; from the musing wood,
And every rock, a life renewed
Exhaled like an unconscious thought
When poets, dreaming unperplexed,
Dream that they dream of nought.
Nature one hour appears a thing unsexed,
Or to such serene balance brought
That her twin natures cease their sweet alarms,
And sleep in one another's arms.
The sun with resting pulses seems to brood,
And slacken its command
                              upon my unurged blood.

The river has not any care
Its passionless water to the sea to bear;
The leaves have brown content;
The wall to me has freshness like a scent,
And takes half-animate the air,
Making one life with its green moss and stain;
And life with all things seems too perfect blent
For anything of life to be aware.

The very shades on hill, and tree, and plain,
Where they have fallen doze,
                    and where they doze remain.

No hill can idler be than I;
No stone its inter-particled vibration
Investeth with a stiller lie;
No heaven with a more urgent rest betrays
The eyes that on it gaze.
We are too near akin that thou shouldst cheat
Me, Nature, with thy fair deceit.
In poets floating like a water-flower
Upon the bosom of the glassy hour,
In skies that no man sees to move,
Lurk untumultuous vortices of power,
For joy too native, and for agitation
Too instant, too entire for sense thereof,
Motion like gnats when autumn suns are low,
Perpetual as the prisoned feet of love
On the heart's floors with painèd pace that go.
From stones and poets you may know,
Nothing so active is, as that which least seems so.

For he, that conduit running wine of song,
Then to himself does most belong
When he his mortal house unbars
To the importunate and thronging feet
That round our corporal walls unheeded beat;
Till, all containing, he exalt
His stature to the stars, or stars
Narrow their heaven to his fleshy vault:
When, like a city under ocean,
To human things he grows a desolation,
And is made a habitation
For the fluctuous universe
To lave with unimpeded motion.

He scarcely frets the atmosphere
With breathing, and his body shares
The immobility of rocks;
His heart's a drop-well of tranquillity;
His mind more still is than the limbs of fear,
And yet its unperturbed velocity
The spirit of the simoom mocks.
He round the solemn centre of his soul
Wheels like a dervish, while his being is
Streamed with the set of the world's harmonies,
In the long draft of whatsoever sphere
He lists the sweet and clear
Clangour of his high orbit on to roll,
So gracious is his heavenly grace;
And the bold stars does hear,
Every one in his airy soar,
For evermore
Shout to each other from the peaks of space,
As 'thwart ravines of azure
                    shouts the mountaineer.
                              Francis Thompson (1859-1907)

— 40 —

AN AUTUMN GARDEN

My tent stands in a garden
Of aster and golden-rod,
Tilled by the rain and the sunshine,
And sown by the hand of God,—
An old New England pasture
Abandoned to peace and time,
And by the magic of beauty
Reclaimed to the sublime.

About it are golden woodlands
Of tulip and hickory;
On the open ridge behind it
You may mount to a glimpse of sea,—
The far-off, blue, Homeric
Rim of the world's great shield,
A border of boundless glamour
For the soul's familiar field.

In purple and grey-wrought lichen
The boulders lie in the sun;
Along its grassy footpath,
The white-tailed rabbits run.
The crickets work and chirrup
Through the still afternoon;
And the owl calls at twilight
Under the frosty moon.

The odorous wild grape clambers
Over the tumbling wall,
And through the autumnal quiet
The chestnuts open and fall.
Sharing time's freshness and fragrance,
Part of the earth's great soul

Here man's spirit may ripen
To wisdom serene and whole.

Shall we not grow with the asters?—
Never reluctant nor sad,
Not counting the cost of being,
Living to dare and be glad.
Shall we not lift with the crickets
A chorus or ready cheer,
Braving the frost of oblivion,
Quick to be happy here?

The deep red cones of the sumach
And the woodbine's crimson sprays
Have bannered the common roadside
For the pageant of passing days.
These are the oracles Nature
Fills with her holy breath,
Giving them glory of colour,
Transcending the shadow of death.

Here in the sifted sunlight
A spirit seems to brood
On the beauty and worth of being,
In tranquil, instinctive mood
And the heart, athrob with gladness
Such as the wise earth knows,
Wells with a full thanksgiving
For the gifts that life bestows:

For the ancient and virile nurture
Of the teeming primordial ground,
For the splendid gospel of colour,
The rapt revelations of sound;
For the morning-blue above us
And the rusted gold of the fern,
For the chickadee's call to valour
Bidding the faint-heart turn;

For fire and running water,
Snowfall and summer rain;
For sunsets and quiet meadows,
The fruit and the standing grain;
For the solemn hour of moonrise
Over the crest of trees,
When the mellow lights are kindled
In the lamps of the centuries.

For those who wrought aforetime,
Led by the mystic strain
To strive for the larger freedom,
And live for the greater gain;
For plenty and peace and playtime,
The homely goods of earth,
And for rare immaterial treasures
Accounted of little worth;

For art and learning and friendship,
Where beneficent truth is supreme,
Those everlasting cities
Built on the hills of dream;
For all things growing and goodly
That foster this life, and breed
The immortal flower of wisdom
Out of the mortal seed.

But most of all for the spirit
That can not rest nor bide
In stale and sterile convenience,
Nor safety proven and tried,
But still inspired and driven,
Must seek what better may be,
And up from the loveliest garden
Must climb for a glimpse of sea.

Bliss Carman (1861-1929)

— 41 —

GRAY ON ENGLISH GARDENS

*He (Count Algarotti) is highly civil to our nation but there is one
little point, in which he does not do us justice. I am the more
solicitous about it, because it relates to the only taste which we can
call our own, the only proof of our original talent in matter of
pleasure; I mean, our skill in gardening and laying out grounds.
That the Chinese have this beautiful art in high perfection, seems
very probable . . . but it is very certain we copied nothing from
them, nor had anything but nature for our model . . .*

Thomas Gray to William Taylor Howe (1763).

ELEGY WRITTEN IN A COUNTRY CHURCH-YARD

The Curfew tolls the knell of parting day,
The lowing herd wind slowly o'er the lea,
The ploughman homeward plods his weary way,
And leaves the world to darkness and to me.

Now fades the glimmering landscape on the sight,
And all the air a solemn stillness holds,
Save where the beetle wheels his droning flight,
And drowsy tinklings lull the distant folds

Save that from yonder ivy-mantled tow'r
The moping owl does to the moon complain
Of such, as wand'ring near her secret bow'r,
Molest her ancient solitary reign.

Beneath those rugged elms, that yew-tree's shade,
Where heaves the turf in many a mould'ring heap,
Each in his narrow cell for ever laid,
The rude Forefathers of the hamlet sleep.

The breezy call of incense-breathing Morn,
The swallow twitt'ring from the straw-built shed,
The cock's shrill clarion, or the echoing horn,
No more shall rouse them from their lowly bed.

For them no more the blazing hearth shall burn,
Or busy housewife ply her evening care:
No children run to lisp their sire's return,
Or climb his knees the envied kiss to share.

Oft did the harvest to their sickle yield,
Their furrow oft the stubborn glebe has broke
How jocund did they drive their team afield !
How bow'd the woods beneath their sturdy stroke

Let not Ambition mock their useful toil,
Their homely joys, and destiny obscure;
Nor Grandeur hear with a disdainful smile,
The short and simple annals of the poor.

The boast of heraldry, the pomp of pow'r,
And all that beauty, all that wealth e'er gave,
Awaits alike th' inevitable hour.
The paths of glory lead but to the grave.

Nor you, ye Proud, impute to These the fault,
If Mem'ry o'er their Tomb no Trophies raise,
Where thro' the long-drawn isle and fretted vault
The pealing anthem swells the note of praise.

Can storied urn or animated bust
Back to its mansion call the fleeting breath?
Can Honour's voice provoke the silent dust,
Or Flatt'ry sooth the dull cold ear of Death?

Perhaps in this neglected spot is laid
Some heart once pregnant with celestial fire
Hands, that the rod of empire might have sway'd,
Or wak'd to extasy the living tyre.

But Knowledge to their eyes her ample page
Rich with the spoils of time did ne'er unroll
Chill Penury repress'd their noble rage,
And froze the genial current of the soul.

Full many a gem of purest ray serene,
The dark unfathom'd caves of ocean bear:
Full many a flower is born to blush unseen,
And waste its sweetness on the desert air.

Some village-Hampden, that with dauntless breast
The little Tyrant of his fields withstood
Some mute inglorious Milton here may rest,
Some Cromwell guiltless of his country's blood.

Th' applause of list'ning senates to command.
The threats of pain and ruin to despise,
To scatter plenty o'er a smiling land,
And read their hist'ry in a nation's eyes,

Their lot forbad : nor circumscrib'd alone
Their growing virtues, but their crimes confin'd
Forbad to wade through slaughter to a throne,
And shut the gates of mercy on mankind,

The struggling pangs of conscious truth to hide,
To quench the blushes of ingenuous shame,
Or heap the shrine of Luxury and Pride
With incense kindled at the Muse's flame.

Far from the madding crowd's ignoble strife,
Their sober wishes never learn'd to stray;
Along the cool sequester'd vale of life
They kept the noiseless tenor of their way.

Yet ev'n these bones from insult to protect
Some trail memorial still erected nigh,
With uncouth rhimes and shapeless sculpture deck'd,
Implores the passing tribute of a sigh.

Their name, their years, spelt by th' unletter'd muse,
The place of fame and elegy supply:
And many a holy text around she strews,
That teach the rustic moralist to die.

For who to dumb Forgetfulness a prey,
This pleasing anxious being e'er resign'd,
Left the warm precincts of the cheerful day,
Nor cast one longing ling'ring look behind?

On some fond breast the parting soul relics,
Some pious drops the closing eye requires;
Ev'n from the tomb the voice of Nature cries,
Ev'n in our Ashes live their wonted Fires.

For thee, who mindful of th' unhonour'd Dead
Dost in these lines their artless tale relate;
If chance, by lonely contemplation led,
Some kindred Spirit shall inquire thy fate,

Haply some hoary-headed Swain may say,
'Oft have we seen him at the peep of dawn
Brushing with hasty steps the dears away
To meet the sun upon the upland lawn.

There at the foot of yonder nodding beech
That wreathes its old fantastic roots so high,
His listless length at noontide would he stretch,
And pore upon the brook that babbles by.

Hard by yon wood, now smiling as in scorn,
Mutt'ring his wayward fancies he would rove,
Now drooping, woeful wan, like one forlorn,
Or craz'd with care, or cross'd in hopeless love.

One morn I miss'd him on the custom'd hill,
Along the heath and near his fav'rite tree;
Another came; nor yet beside the rill,
Nor up the lawn, nor at the wood was he;

The next with dirges due in sad array
Slow thro' the church-way path we saw him born.
Approach and read (for thou can'st read) the lay,
Grav'd on the stone beneath yon aged thorn'.

THE EPITAPH

Here rests his head upon the lap of Earth
A Youth to Fortune and to Fame unknown.
Fair Science frown'd not on his humble birth,
And Melancholy mark'd him for her own.

Large was his bounty, and his soul sincere,
Heav'n did a recompense as largely send:
He gave to Mis'ry all he had, a tear,
He gain'd from Heav'n ('twas all he wish'd) a friend.

No farther seek his merits to disclose
Or draw his frailties from their dread abode,
(There they alike in trembling hope repose,)
The bosom of his Father and his God.

Thomas Gray (1716-1771)

— 42 —

ODE ON SOLITUDE

Happy the man, whose wish and care
    A few paternal acres bound,
Content to breathe his native air
        In his own ground.

Whose herds with milk, whose fields with bread,
    Whose flocks supply him with attire;
Whose trees in summer yield him shade,
        In winter fire.

Blest! who can unconcern'dly find
    Hours, days, and years slide soft away
In health of body, peace of mind,
        Quiet by day,

Sound sleep by night; study and ease
    Together mix'd; sweet recreation,
And innocence, which most does please
        With meditation.

Thus let me live, unseen, unknown;
    Thus unlamented let me die;
Steal from the world, and not a stone
        Tell where I lie.

Alexander Pope (1688-1744)

— 43 —

IN A QUIET GARDEN

When I walked in the Lenten garden
The buds on the trees were as hard
As the stones of the path at my feet
Or the stone hid in my heart.

Then I walked in the Passiontide Garden
With Gethsemane still in my heart;
The buds were beginning to break —
Yet all I could find was a tomb
Sealed with a greater stone.

But again I walked in the Garden
And I saw how the trees were in bloom;
Shrine for an empty tomb
With the stone rolled away —
And the stone in my heart was raised
By the promise of Easter Day.

(Brigid Boardman)

— 44 —

PRAYER

Be not afraid to pray — to pray is right.
Pray, if thou canst, with hope; but ever pray,
Though hope be weak, or sick with long delay;
Pray in the darkness if there be no light.
Far is the time, remote from human sight,
When war and discord on the earth shall cease;
Yet every prayer for universal peace
Avails the blessed time to expedite.

Whate'er is good to wish, ask that of Heaven,
Though it be what thou can'st not hope to see;
Pray to be perfect, though material leaven
Forbid the spirit so on earth to be:
But if for any wish thou darest not pray,
Then pray to God to cast that wish away.

Hartley Coleridge (1796-1849)

— 45 —

INVERSNAID

This darksome burn, horseback brown,
His rollrock highroad roaring down,
In coop and in comb the fleece of his foam
Flutes and low to the lake falls home.

A windpuff-bonnet of fáwn-fróth
Turns and twindles over the broth
Of a pool so pitchblack, féll-frówning,
It rounds and rounds Despair to drowning.

Degged with dew, dappled with dew
Are the groins of the braes that the brook
                                        treads through,
Wiry heathpacks, flitches of fern,
And the beadbonny ash that sits over the burn.

What would the world be, once bereft
Of wet and of wildness? Let them be left,
O let them be left, wildness and wet;
Long live the weeds and the wilderness yet.

Gerard Manley Hopkins

NOTES

1. Jer. 31: 11-12.
2. Isaiah 58: 11.
3. Song 4: 12.
4. Song 4: 16.
5. Song 5: 1.
6: John 15: 4-6.
7: *Early Christian Writers*, 1968, pp.183-4.
8: *Letters of St. Paulinus of Nola*, 2 vols. *Ancient Christian, Writers*, 35, 36, 1967 Vol. 2, p.200..
9. *Works of Saint Teresa*, trans. E Allison Peers, 3 vols. 1946. I. pp.65; 86-7.
10. Francis Quarles, *The School of the Heart*, 1647, reprinted *c*.1888.
11. Gen. 2: 8-9; 15.
12. The author is indebted to Sara Covin Juengst for these translations from the Hebrew. See: *Like a Garden*, 1996, p.41.
13. Psalm 65: 9-10. [64: 10-11]
14. Psalm 104.[103]: 14-17.
15. Isaiah 51: 3.
16. Isaiah 55: 10-11.
17. Matt. 15: 13
18. *Meditations with Hildegard of Bingen,* edited by Gabriele Uhlein, 1983, pp.77-80.
19. From the Office of Readings for the Feast of the Immaculate Conception (8th December).
20. Hildegard of Bingen, *Book of Divine Work, with Letters and Songs,* edited by Matthew Fox, 1987, p.379.
21. *The Poems of Gerard Manley Hopkins*, edited by W.H.Gardner & N.H.Mackenzie, 1967, pp.76-78
22. Eleanor Farjeon, 'Morning Has Broken', Hymn 196, *Complete Celebration Hymnal*, 1984.
23. Siegfried Sassoon, 'The Heart's Journey': III, *Collected Poems*, 1947, p.176.

24. Caryll Houselander, 'A Tree in the City', *The Flowering Tree*, 1973, pp.22-23.

25. M. Aumonier, 'Sun and Shade', *The Poetry of Gardens*, 1928, p.18.

26. George Herbert, 'The Flower', *The Christian Poetry Collection*, compiled by Mary Batchelor, 1995, pp.162-63.

27. Edward Hayes, 'Autumn'. Untraced, but a version of this poem entitled 'Autumn Psalm of Contentment' is quoted in *Earth Prayers* edited by Elizabeth Roberts and Elias Amidon, p.314-315.

28. Gabriele Uhlein, *Meditations with Hildegard of Bingen,* op.cit., p.60.

29. William Shakespeare, Sonnet 73, *The Sonnets*, Penguin edition, 1964, p.113.

30. Pierre Teilhard de Chardin, *Le Milieu Divin*, 1960, pp.59; 61.

31. Frances Hodgson Burnett, *The Secret Garden* (1911), 1998, pp.61-64.

32. Thomas Tusser, *Five Hundred Points of Good Husbandry* (1580), 1984, pp.94-95.

33. Urban T. Holmes, quoted in Carolyn Huffman, *Meditations in a Rose Garden*, 1995, p.45.

34. Rudyard Kipling, 'The Glory of the Garden', *Selected Poems*, 1993, pp.147-48.

35. W.B.Yeats, 'The Lake Isle of Innisfree', *Collected Poems*, 1952, p.44.

36. C.Forrest McDowell & T.Clark McDowell, *The Sanctuary Garden*, 1998, pp.21; 27

37. Andrew Marvell, 'The Garden', *The Poems of Andrew Marvell*, 1953, pp.51-52.

38. From the Office of readings for Holy Saturday.

39. Mary Coleridge, 'When Mary Thro' the Garden Went', *Christian Poetry Collection*, compiled by Mary Batchelor, 1995, p.316.

40. Francis Thompson, 'The Kingdom of God', *Poems of Francis Thompson*, 1941, p.293.

41.   Gen. 22.

42.   Gen. 28.

43.   Gen. 32.

44.   Tobit.

45.   Dan. 3

46.   *The Book of Paradise*, translated by E.Wallis Budge. 2 vols. 1904, I: p.145.

47.   Saint Peter Damian, Letter to Saint Hugh of Semur. *PL.*, cxliv.

48.   Walafrid Strabo, *Hortulus*, Dedication, 6-15. Trans. E. Lambert as *The Little Garden*, 1924.

49.   William Langland, *Piers Plowman*, edited by W.W.Skeat. *EETS* o.s. 38, 1869, p.158.

50.   Thomas of Celano, *The Lives of Saint Francis of Assisi,* edited by A.G.Ferrers Howell, 1908, p.297.

51.   Aelred of Riveaux, *Amicitia Christiana*, translated by Hugh Talbot as *Christian Friendship*, 1942, p.96.

52.   E.Nesbit, 'The Grey-Walled Garden', *A Little Light Weeding*, edited by Richard Briers, 1994, p.157.

53.   Michael Mayne, *This Sunrise of Wonder*, 1995, p.29.

54.   Thomas Traherne, *Centuries of Meditations*, (1908), 1960, p.109.

55.   T.S.Eliot, 'Burnt Norton', *Collected Poems*, 1963, pp.189-190.

56.   Translation from 'Early English Magic and Medicine' by Charles Singer, *Proceedings of the British Academy* IV. Quoted by Eleanour Sinclair Rhode in *The Old English Herbals*, 1971, pp.40-41.

57.   Peter Walton, 'The Allotment'. Quoted by D.Crouch & C.Ward, *The Allotment, its Landscape and Culture*, 1997, p.187.

58.   David Hassler & Lynn Gregor, *A Place to Grow*, 1998, pp.9-11.

59.   Hildegard of Bingen, *Gifts from Hildegard*, edited by Wanda Nash, 1997, p.45.

60.   William Blake, *Complete Writings*, 1966, p.431.

61. Rainer Maria Rilke, 'I find you, Lord, in all things', in *The Book of Hours — Selected Poetry of Rainer Maria Rilke*, 1989, p.5.

62. Antoine de Saint-Exupéry, *The Little Prince*, (1943), 1971, p.77.

63. Rosemary Sutcliffe, *Blue Remembered Hills: A Recollection*, 1983, p.132.

64. R.S.Thomas, 'The Bright Field', *Laboratories of the Spirit*, quoted by Michael Mayne in *This Sunrise of Wonder*, 1995, p.275.

65. Francis Thompson, 'An Anthem of Earth', lines 184-192. op.cit. p.222.

ACKNOWLEDGEMENTS

The publishers acknowledge the extant copyright of several quotations in Part I of *In a Quiet Garden* and are grateful for the permissions which have been given for reproduction: Faber and Faber Ltd for the poem 'Burnt Norton' by T.S.Eliot (from *Collected Poems 1909-1962*). Barbara Levy Literary Agency for an extract from *The Heart's Journey* by Siegfried Sassoon. Quotations from *Meditations with Hildegard of Bingen* by Gabriele Uhlein, copyright 1983, reprinted with permission of Bear & Co., Santa Fe, NM. David Higham Associates for 'Morning has Broken' by Eleanor Farjeon extracted from *The Children's Bells* (Oxford University Press). HarperCollins Publishers Ltd for extracts from *The Sunrise of Wonder* by Michael Mayne. B.M.Boardman for the illustrations and for her poem 'In a Quiet Garden'. The Pilgrim Press, Cleveland, Ohio, for the text of Fr Jim O'Donell quoted in D.Hassler & L.Gregor's *A Place to Grow*. Mr R.S.Thomas for his poem 'The Bright Field' (see n.64). Bodley Head for a quotation from the writings of Rosemary Sutcliffe (see n.63). Sheed & Ward for a quotation from the writings of Caryll Houselander (see n.24). Editions du Seuil, Paris, for a quotation from *Le Milieu Divin* by Pierre Teilhard de Chardin.The assistence of Heinemann Publishers (Oxford); HarperCollins; Robson Books; Faber & Faber Ltd and Westminster John Knox Press in tracing other copyright holders is also acknowledged. While every effort has been made to contact holders of copyright, any who have not been included in the above list are invited to apply to the publishers who will be pleased to credit them in full in any subsequent editions.

THE QUIET GARDEN MOVEMENT

The primary vision of The Quiet Garden Movement is to encourage a network of local opportunities for silence and reflection.

The Quiet Garden Trust is a Registered Charity which seeks to seed and support a ministry of Christians from mainstream churches who have organized low-cost retreats in people's homes and gardens. The ministry is grounded in the Christian tradition of prayer.

The Trust believes that there is a need for a variety of reflective experiences to inform and balance human activity. It meets this need by helping to establish and resource places for prayer, silence, reflection, the appreciation of beauty, learning about Christian spirituality and experiencing creativity and healing in the context of God's love.

A Quiet Garden comes into being when someone responds to the vision of the Trust and agrees to open their garden for occasional days of reflection and stillness. They have been established all over the world and are increasingly coming to fruition in schools, colleges, hospitals, retreat centres, monasteries and religious institutes in addition to the many, often quite small, private gardens.

The pattern of a Quiet Day is very flexible and it is important that all visitors feel relaxed and free to use the time as they wish. They are at liberty to arrive and depart at any time during the day, respecting the quiet which other people may be enjoying. Most people wish to be silent from the initial welcome onwards.

As one of the Patrons wrote recently: *". . . Quiet Gardens are a glorious way of responding to the clear message of Jesus, demonstrated by his choosing to withdraw regularly from the hurly-burly of everyday life, into a natural setting, to focus on his communion with God. In the Quiet Garden ministry we share in God's creative work, by enabling people to find rest, to pray, to receive spiritual nurture and healing, to rediscover their true path and, as a result, to become more concerned for this creation."*

Enquiries about using or establishing a Quiet Garden are always welcomed by the Trust at:
    Stoke Park Farm, Park Road, Stoke Poges, Bucks SL2 4PG
Tel: 01753 643050   Fax: 643081 E-mail: quiet.garden@ukonline.co.uk
Director: The Rev Philip Roderick   Assistant Director: Mrs Jackie Lock

Look, what thy memory cannot contain
Commit to these waste blanks, and thou shalt find
Those children nurs'd deliver'd from thy brain,
To take a new acquaintance of thy mind.
　　　These offices, so oft as thou wilt look,
　　　Shall profit thee, and much enrich thy book.
William Shakespeare (1564-1616)